Guide to the identification of
ALFA ROMEO CARS

Maurizio Tabucchi

Guide to the identification of
ALFA ROMEO CARS

GIORGIO NADA EDITORE

Giorgio Nada Editore s.r.l.

Editorial coordination, cover and graphics
Giorgio Nada Editore

Translation
Robert Newman

With few exceptions, the photographs in this book were provided by the Documentation Centre of Alfa Romeo.

Acknowledgements
The author wishes to thank all those who helped make this book possible, especially:
- Roberto Guarini
Director of Product and Brand Policy, Alfa Romeo.
- Stefano D'Amico
President of the Alfa Romeo Register, Italy.
- Elvira Ruocco
Head of the Historical Documentation Centre, Alfa Romeo, and keeper of the Italian Alfa Romeo Register, for her unfailing collaboration.
- Paolo Bezzan
Homologation office, Alfa Romeo, for his indispensable assistance.

In addition, sincere thanks to Maurizio Forleo and Lorenzo Marzullo for their contribution to the final draft of this book.

Giorgio Nada Editore
Via Claudio Treves, 15/17
I – 20090 VIMODRONE MI
Tel. +39 02 27301126
Fax +39 02 27301454
E-mail: nadamail@work-net.it
http://www.giorgionadaeditore.it

The catalogue of Giorgio Nada Editore publications is available on request at the address above.

Guide to the Identification of Alfa Romeo Cars
ISBN: 88-7911-233-3

Distributed in the USA and Canada by
MBI Publishing Company
729 Prospect Avenue, PO Box 1,
Osceola, WI 54020-0001, USA

GUIDE TO THE IDENTIFICATION OF THE PRODUCTION OF ALFA ROMEO CARS

1910 – 1986

INTRODUCTION

The objective of this book is to bring together all the A.L.F.A., Alfa Romeo and Alfasud cars sold in Italy, plus the most important models sold overseas, using pictures of the period which are, therefore, historically accurate; in a very few cases, photographs have been used of carefully selected cars which have been either preserved or restored.

Racing cars not available to the public but used by works drivers have been excluded, although mention has been made of them at the end of each annual section; they will be the subject of a subsequent publication. An Alfa Romeo story which is presented in this way, recording the appearance of new models year-by-year and which indicates modifications made to cars already in production, may seem cold and schematic and, therefore, more distant than others which are more conventional.

But in this way, using a system of consultation which can be immediately understood, I wanted to provide answers to the more frequent questions posed by students of the brand, potential buyers of vintage Alfa Romeo cars and enthusiasts.

Thanks to the amount of historical and technical data and with a series of comparative information and elements which can be easily verified, it is particularly easy to identify each Alfa Romeo and personally evaluate the conformity of the various components.

I considered it appropriate to bring this project to a close for the moment with the introduction of front-wheel drive, also on the traditional Alfa Romeos.

The Author

Above left the first A.L.F.A. badge: right, the badge introduced in 1925 after winning the first world championship.

CONSULTATION GUIDE

The official production registers – in which every Alfa Romeo car ever made was recorded by hand and given progressive engine and chassis numbers – were either destroyed in a bombing raid on 20 October, 1944, or lost at a later date. Therefore, the company was only able to provide me with exact production information dating from 1942 onwards.

However, as a result of painstaking research, its has been possible to fill in many of the gaps, even though retaining some doubts concerning the numerical sequence and dating of some cars.

This publication provides a start and finish of chassis and engine numbers of all cars sold to the public and does, as far as it can, constitute above all a guide to the purchase of a vintage Alfa Romeo. This has been achieved by consulting official registers kept in the historical archives of the company.

As well as listing in chronological order the principal variants of a basic car project, I have also included a description of the more significant technical and aesthetic modifications carried out during the production cycle of every single model.

I have also indicated the bodies most frequently produced, or at least those which are known today. However, it should be pointed out that it was not until 1930 that Alfa Romeo started to manufacture bodies themselves. Until that time, the company restricted itself to making chassis on which outside companies built the bodies.

As well as enabling the precise verification of correspondence between apparently similar components but which were made in different periods, this book facilitates the establishment of the exact date of each car.

Possible discordance with the date of registration can be attributed to lateness due stocking and the unavailability of a certain model and delay in delivery, but that does not affect the dating process.

It is also possible to note discrepancies between the official date of presentation of some models and the start of their production which can, in some cases, even result in a car being dated a year earlier.

The official denomination of each model, which is expressed in heavier type, is the result of a careful study aimed at avoiding unofficial definitions or at least those not envisaged by the company. This was achieved by basing the research on original documentation: registers of production, homologation forms, instruction and maintenance manuals, original designs and spare parts catalogues.

Do not be surprised by denominations such as T.I. in capital or small letters with or without full stops between them, or the term Turbodiesel written in upper or lower case letters, separated (Turbo Diesel) or expressed as TD. All of this comes from a meticulous study of the official denominations, which were not always consistent but which I decided to faithfully reproduce.

It should be pointed out that, from 1900 onwards, the identification code (type) coincides with the code of usage for the homologation of models by Italy's I.G.M. (General Inspectorate of Civil Motorisation and Transport in Concession) in the beginning and later by the D.G.M. (the General Management of Civil Motorisation). The annotation of chassis and engine type does not appear on models produced before the Second World War because, except in very rare cases, the pre-war data always coincided with the denomination of the model.

Power output is expressed in DIN horse power (15% less than SAE, in line with a rule which Alfa Romeo always respected).

From 1950, when left-hand drive was generalised with the launch of the 1900, it was decided to indicate only the significant right-hand drive conversions, rarely sold in Italy, with a different identification code.

Variations which were just formal – relative to export models as a result of the different equipment which the traffic regulations of various countries imposed – even if only characterised by specific code designations and, more recently, also by commercial denominations which are completely different, have been omitted. In the same way, certain model variants were omitted (33 Imola, 33 Privilège, 33 Absolute etc) which appeared in particular after 1980. They were built on identical chassis mentioned earlier in official lists or destined for overseas markets: changes mainly concerned aesthetics and in no way influenced performance.

In the case of technical or aesthetic modifications not officialised by the company through variations of the identification code (type) or the use of a new numbering system, the numerical sequence of the chassis produced in that year counts for both versions

The Author

1910

24 HP (SERIES A)

4 cylinders in line, 4082 cc, 42 hp, single camshaft in crankcase.
Wheelbase 3020 mm and 3200 mm.

Chassis for:

DOUBLE PHAETON,
LAUDAULET COUPE' DE
VILLE, LIMOUSINE,
TOURER,...

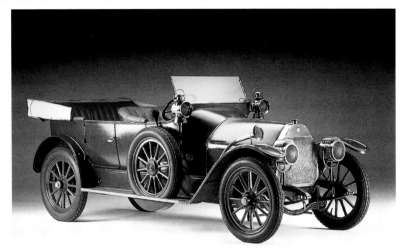

Conceived by Giuseppe Merosi in 1909 for the Società Italiana Automobili Darracq headed by Cav. Ugo Stella, the new car revealed itself so modern (single block engine and transmission with universal joint) that, when evolved into the **20-30 HP** version, it represented in 1921 a valid basis from which to begin the construction of the **20/30 E.S. Sport**. The chassis was of longitudinal steel side members with cross-beams, a solution which was adopted – even if with many modifications – until as late as 1950. The suspension was constituted of semi-elliptic leaf springs front and rear at $^3/_4$ ellipse, the front and rear axles were rigid.

Beaded tyres *815 x 105 front (on request 820 x 120); 820 x 120 rear. **Chassis and engines from 601 to 615.**

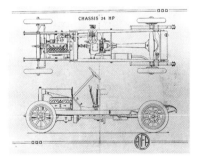

12 HP (SERIES A)

4 cylinders in line, 2413 cc, 22 hp, single camshaft in crankcase. Wheelbase 2779 mm.

Chassis for:

DOUBLE PHAETON,
LANDAULET, LIMOUSINE,
TOURER,...

Another of Merosi's creations with similar characteristics to the **24 HP**, less complex but with an equally sporting temperament, the **12 HP** was born at almost the same time as the **24 HP.**
Beaded tyres* 810 x 90. Three speed gearbox.
With these characteristics, the car did well in the First Modena Regularity Race (Primo Concorso di Regolarità di Modena) in 1911 (five laps for a total of 1500 kms), the first race in which Alfa took part and in which the need for a number of improvements, incorporated in the Series B, was recognised. **Chassis and engines from 1001 to 1050 (until 1911).**

14-16 HP

4 cylinders in line, 2269 cc, single camshaft in crankcase. Wheelbase 2520 mm.

Chassis for:

DOUBLE PHAETON,
FIACRE (TAXI),
LANDAULET,...

Even if they have no reference which can attribute them to A.L.F.A. and, therefore, are still attributable to Darracq, some of the original designs for this small car, with its much reduced wheelbase and racing engine of relatively short bore (85 x 100), kept in the Alfa Romeo historic archives are dated 13.7.1910, meaning they were produced when A.L.F.A. had already been established and Darracq had ceased to operate.

The presence of an illustrated leaflet of the period which, however, defines the vehicle as model **15 HP**, suggests that the **14-16 HP**, a project which also included the production of a taxi (hackney cab) but did not go ahead, was sold as the economical version of the **15 HP**, an alternative to a similar model unveiled in 1912 with a capacity of 2413 cc, a wheelbase of 2864 mm and a four speed gearbox.

But an interesting point, which invalidates the hypothesis that it could have been a project conceived at Suresnes and that it was immediately abandoned in Milan, is the fact that the drawings are signed by Antonio Santoni, Giuseppe Merosi's designer and right hand man. The last drawing, dated as late as 3 April, 1912, describes a modification to be carried out to the differential.

Beaded tyres* 810 x 90, three speed gearbox.
Chassis and engine numbers unknown.

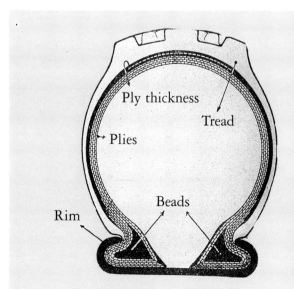

Ply thickness

Tread

Plies

Beads

Rim

*At the time when A.L.F.A. was created (1910), the only tyre available was the so-called beaded type and, as a result, rims had to be in C-shaped sections which clamped the beads, part of the one-piece tyre with an inner tube. The inflation pressure had to be very high – around 4 bar - because it was only then that the tyre stayed on the rim. Beaded tyres remained in use until the late Twenties, when they were replaced by grooved tyres, the basic principle of which is still in use today.

From 1907, anyway, tyres with straight beads were used with what were called straight side rims (see the 1027 note). These were not widely used in Europe except from the late Twenties, but when they appeared in the U.S.A. they almost completely substituted beaded rims.

1911

24 HP (SERIES B)

4 cylinders in line, 4082 cc, 42 hp, single camshaft in crankcase. Wheelbase 3020 mm.

Chassis for:

DOUBLE PHAETON, LANDAULET, COUPE' DE VILLE, LIMOUSINE TOURER,...

Production of the long chassis was abandoned.
Beaded tyres 815x105 front (on request 820x120); 820x120 rear.
Leaf springs front, semi-elliptic rear with 3/4 ellipse.
Chassis and engines from 616 to 650.

NO SIGNIFICANT MODIFICATIONS TO THE FOLLOWING MODELS:
12 HP (Series A). Chassis and engine included in 1910 numbering.
14-16 HP. Chassis and engine numbers not available.

COMPETITION CAR NOT FOR PUBLIC SALE
24 HP - RACING TYPE TWO BUCKET SEATS

1912

24 HP (SERIES C)

4 cylinders in line, 4082 cc, 45 hp, single camshaft in crankcase. Wheelbase 3020 mm

Chassis for:

DOUBLE PHAETON,
LANDAULET, COUPE',
DE VILLE, LIMOUSINE,
TOURER,...

Power was increased by 3 HP.
During the year, the rear leaf springs with 3/4 ellipse were replaced by semi-elliptics.
All other technical characteristics remained unchanged.
Beaded tyres 815x105 front (on request 820x120); 820x120 rear.
Chassis and engines from 651 to 804.

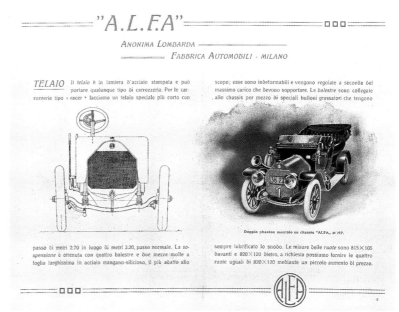

A leaflet of the period describing the 24 HP's technical characteristics.

15 HP (SERIES B)

4 cylinders in line, 2413 cc, 25 hp, single camshaft in crankcase. Wheelbase 2864 mm.

Chassis for:

DOUBLE PHAETON,
LANDAULET, LIMOUSINE,
TOURER,...

Following the result obtained in the Concorso di Modena a year earlier, power was increased and the car's designation was changed from **12 HP** to **15 HP**.
The wheelbase was increased by 8.5 cm, a four speed gearbox was introduced as were a multiple disc clutch and a brake on the transmission operated by a hand lever.
Beaded tyres 760x90 (on request 810x90).
Chassis and engine from 1051 to 1150 (until 1913).

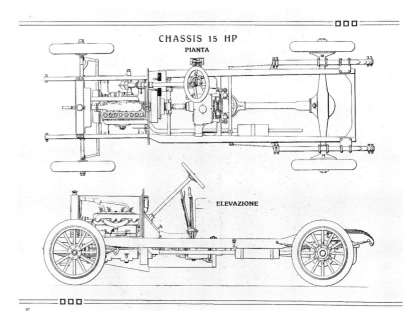

1913

24 HP (SERIES D)

4 cylinders in line, 4082 cc, 45 hp, single camshaft in crankcase. Wheelbase 3200 mm.

Chassis for:

DOUBLE PHAETON.
LANDAULET, COUPE'
DE VILLE, LIMOUSINE
TOURER,…

The company returned to a long wheelbase of 3200mm. Technical characteristics remained the same as for the Series C.
Leaf springs front and semi-elliptics rear.
Beaded tyres 815x105 front (820x120 on request); 820x120 rear.
Chassis and engine from 805 to 902 (including 1914 production).

An advertisement of the period featuring the 24 HP Series D, the A.L.F.A. badge, Portillo factory and the Milan cathedral.

40-60 HP (SERIES A)

4 cylinders in line, 6082 cc, 70 hp, twin camshafts in crankcase. Wheelbase 3200 mm.

The Ricotti Torpedo

Chassis for:

DOUBLE PHAETON,
LANDAULET, COUPE' DE
VILLE, LIMOUSINE,
TOURER,…

A six litre engine with overhead valves operated by rods and rocker arms plus twin camshafts in the crankcase made the new car, which completed the A.L.F.A. product range, an unbeatable racing vehicle, even if it was

not intended for competition.
It should be noted that many parts of the chassis came from the **24 HP**. The Torpedo is important from the aerodynamic point of view: bodywork (right) is by Castagna for a pro-

ject by Marco Ricotti: its top speed was 139 km/h compared to the 110 km/h of the normal **40-60 HP**.
Beaded tyres 835 x 135.
Chassis and engine from 2001 to 2028 (until 1915).

NO SIGNIFICANT MODIFICATIONS TO THE FOLLOWING MODELS:
15 hp (Series B). Chassis and engine included in 1912 numbers.

COMPETITION CAR NOT FOR PUBLIC SALE
40-60 HP - RACING TYPE, TWO BUCKET SEATS.

11

1914

15-20 HP (SERIES C)

4 cylinders in line, 2413 cc, 28 hp, single camshaft in crankcase. Wheelbase 2925 mm.

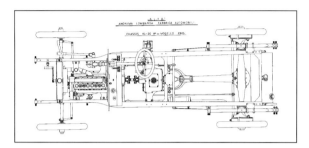 

Chassis for:

DOUBLE PHAETON,
LANDAULET, LIMOUSINE,
TOURER,...

An evolution of the **15 HP** of the same cubic capacity, but with increased power.
Multi-disc clutch. The track was increased by 5 mm and the wheelbase by about 60 mm. The rear leaf springs had 3/4 ellipse.
Beaded tyres 810x90 (760x90 on request).
Chassis and engine from 1151 to 1322 (until 1919).

20-30 HP (SERIES E)

4 cylinders in line, 4082 cc, 49 hp, single camshaft in crankcase. Wheelbase 3200 mm.

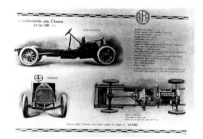

Chassis for:

TORPEDO, LIMOUSINE,
LANDAULET, ROADSTER,...

This was an evolution of the **24 HP**; distribution by the gears was modified by fitting silent chains and power was increased by 4 hp. Some of the material, which was the same as the **24 HP**, was set aside the following year with the outbreak of the First World War but would be used in 1921 for the new **20-30 E.S. Sport**. Beaded tyres 820x120.
Chassis and engine from 3001 to 3280.

> **NO SIGNIFICANT MODIFICATIONS TO THE FOLLOWING MODELS:**
> **24 HP (Series D).** Chassis and engines included in 1913 numbers.
> **40-60 HP (Series A).** Chassis and engines included in the 1913 numbers.

COMPETITION CAR NOT FOR PUBLIC SALE
GRAND PRIX 1914 - TWO SEATER GRAND PRIX CAR
ONLY ONE CAR PRODUCED

1915

NO SIGNIFICANT MODIFICATIONS TO THE FOLLOWING MODELS
15-20 HP (Series C). Chassis and engines from 1151 to 1322 (until 1919).
20-30 HP (Series E). Chassis and engines from 3281 to 3380 (until 1921).
40-60 HP (Series A). Chassis and engines included in 1913 numbers.

1916

Moto Compressore "MONOBLOCCO ROMEO"

IL PIÙ PERFETTO
— IL PIÙ PRATICO
GRUPPO GENERATORE
— TRASPORTABILE —
D'ARIA COMPRESSA

SOCIETÀ ANONIMA ITALIANA
ING. NICOLA ROMEO & C. - MILANO
FILIALI: ROMA, Via del Tritone, 108
NAPOLI, Corso Umberto I, 179

NO CARS PRODUCED. THE PLANT WAS CONVERTED TO THE MANUFACTURE OF WAR MATERIALS. THE COMPANY PRODUCED COMPRESSORS USING APPROPRIATELY MODIFIED ENGINES OF THE 24 HP (SHOWN LEFT).

1917

NO CARS PRODUCED. THE PLANT HAD BEEN CONVERTED TO THE MANUFACTURE OF WAR MATERIALS.

1918

NO CARS PRODUCED. THE PLANT HAD BEEN CONVERTED TO THE MANUFACTURE OF WAR MATERIALS.

1919

NO SIGNIFICANT MODIFICATIONS TO THE FOLLOWING MODELS:
15-20 HP (Series C). Chassis and engines from 1323 to 1330 (until 1920).
20-30 HP (Series E). Chassis and engines included in 1915 numbers.

1920

G 1 (SERIES G)

6 cylinders in line, 6330 cc, 70 hp, single camshaft in crankcase. Wheelbase 3400 mm.

Chassis for:

TOURER,
LIMOUSINE,
ROADSTER,...

Initially conceived by Giuseppe Merosi with a 6597 cc engine, which was slightly reduced in cubic capacity and its power increased using different camshaft timing.

The Limousine on display at the 1921 London Motor Show.

The suggestion to produce this car, but more than that the evolution of the engine to include overhead valves for use in competition, came from Enzo Ferrari, who had for some time been an Alfa Romeo works driver and saw considerable racing development possibilities in this project. It was Alfa's intention that the **G1** should be sold alongside the **20-30 E.S. Sport**, but its high class, cubic capacity and consequent notable fuel consumption which was unsustainable so soon after the war, were obstacles that meant production was limited to 52 cars, all of them sold in Australia.

Beaded tyres 895x135.

Chassis and engines from 6001 to 6002 (prototypes).

NO SIGNIFICANT MODIFICATIONS TO THE FOLLOWING MODELS
15-20 HP (Series C). Chassis and engines included in 1919 numbering.
20-30 HP (Series E). Chassis and engines included in 1915 numbering.

COMPETITION CAR NOT FOR PUBLIC SALE
20-30 HP - RACING TYPE 2 AND 4 BUCKET SEATS (DOUBLE IGNITION)
ONLY ONE CAR PRODUCED

20-30 E.S. SPORT (SERIES E SPORT)

4 cylinders in line, 4250 cc, 67 hp, single camshaft in crankcase. Wheelbase 2900 mm.

Per rispondere alle numerose richieste di un tipo di vettura specialmente gradito agli amatori della velocità, abbiamo creato lo Chassis *E. S. Sport* il quale pur conservando le peculiari caratteristiche di robustezza e di resistenza del tipo normale 20-30 HP permette di sfoggiare velocità tali che gli hanno assicurato un vero record di velocità fra le macchine di turismo.

Velocità e resistenza sono infatti le doti caratteristiche dello Chassis *E. S. " Sport "*.

Promotional literature for 20-30 E.S. Sport.

"ALFA - ROMEO„
TIPO SPORT
E. S. 4 CILINDRI
1921

Chassis for:

TOURER, LIMOUSINE,
ROADSTER,...

These cars were produced using the components of the **24 HP**, also used for the **20-30 HP**, but suitably improved. The bore was increased from 100 to 102 mm, the wheelbase was reduced to 2900 mm and the chassis was radically modified. The electrics were fitted with automatic starting and spoked wheels

with large wing nuts were available on request for fast disassembly.
All the modifications and updating were attributed in great part to Antonio Ascari, Alfa's Lombardy sales agent and already a famous racing driver, who became one of the greatest champions of the post-First World War period.
Beaded tyres 820x135.
Chassis and engines from 3313 to 3315 and from 3381 to 3496.

NO SIGNIFICANT MODIFICATIONS TO THE FOLLOWING MODELS:
20-30 HP (Series E). Chassis and engines included in 1915 numbers.
G1 (Series G). Chassis and engines from 6003 to 6052.

COMPETITION CAR NOT FOR PUBLIC SALE
40-60 HP - TWO BUCKET SEATS AND 'TORPEDO' FOR TRACK AND ROAD RACES.

R.L. NORMALE (1st SERIES)

6 cylinders in line, 2916 cc, 56 hp, single camshaft in crankcase. Wheelbase 3440 mm.

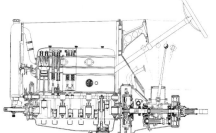

CHASSIS **RL**
6 CILINDRI

Chassis for:

TOURER, LIMOUSINE,
ROADSTER,…

Had the international three litre formula not been reduced to 2000 cc in 1922, the R.L. would have been an optimum basis for a racing car, fitted as it was with a magnificent overhead valve engine, giving it a decidedly sporting character. Even so, it still achieved notable success in its Sport and Super Sport derivatives in road racing for touring cars, right up until the Thirties. "Superflex Cord"* beaded tyres 860x160 or 820x120. **Chassis and engines from 7001 to 7006.**

R.L. SPORT (1st SERIES)

6 cylinders in line, 2994 cc, 71 hp, single camshaft in crankcase. Wheelbase 3140 mm.

Chassis for:

TOURER, LIMOUSINE,
ROADSTER,…

Introduced at the same time as the Normale, but with a greater cubic capacity obtained with an additional bore of 1 mm. An oil radiator was installed. The chassis was shortened to accommodate sports bodies. "Superflex"* beaded tyres 860x160. **Chassis and engines included in R.L. Normale numbers.**

Torpedo sport with Lavezzari body.

NO SIGNIFICANT MODIFICATIONS TO THE FOLLOWING MODEL: 20-30 E.S. Sport (Series E sport). Chassis and engines included in 1921 numbering.

*The purpose of "Superflex" tyres was to minimise the unevenness of the roads of the period; the tyres had very flexible sidewalls and required a lower inflation pressure than the normal beaded cover.
*Instead of layers of fabric laid one on top of the other to form the carcass, the French "Cord" or "Cable" tyres - cord type - had a series of strata of small twisted cords, coated with rubber and laid in criss-cross fashion. This system eliminated the frequent detachment of the fabric layers from each other with consequent lacerations caused by excessive heat build-up.

1923

R.M. NORMALE

4 cylinders in line, 1944 cc, 40 hp, single camshaft in crankcase. Wheelbase 2900 mm.

Chassis for:

TOURER, SALOON
ROADSTER,…

This relatively simple two-litre, four cylinder car used some of the mechanical parts of the R.L. and represented a valid alternative, enabling the company to reduce the cost of conception and production. The size of the bore and stroke were the same as the **R.L. Normale** (75x110); the **R.M.'s** was nothing more than an R.L. engine minus two cylinders. An operation of that kind had already been successfully carried out two years earlier by Fiat with the 505 4 cylinder and 510 6 cylinder models.
Production in 1923 was limited to a few prototypes, one of which was displayed at the Paris Motor Show. Drum brakes on all four wheels. "Superflex" beaded tyres 800x130. **Chassis and engines from 12001 to 12265 until 1924.**

R.L. NORMALE (3rd SERIES)

6 cylinders in line, 2916 cc, 56 hp, single camshaft in crankcase. Wheelbase 3440 mm.

Chassis for:

TOURER, LIMOUSIDE,
ROADSTER,…

The third series embodied a number of mechanical innovations, the most important of which was the introduction in September, 1923, of front brakes. The rears were modified by the elimination of the strap system and expansion brake shoes were adopted. **Chassis and engines from 7351 to 7850.**

R.L. SPORT (3rd SERIES)

6 cylinder, 2994 cc, 71 hp, single camshaft in crankcase. Wheelbase 3140 mm.

Chassis for:

TOURER, LIMOUSINE,
ROADSTER,…

September saw the introduction of front and rear brake shoes in place of those of expansion strap. **Chassis and engines included in R.L. Normale numbers.**

> **NO SIGNIFICANT MODIFICATIONS TO THE FOLLOWING MODELS:**
> **R.L. Normale (2nd Series).** Chassis and engines from 7007 to 7350.
> **R.L. Sport (2nd Series).** Chassis and engines included in the R.L. Normale 2nd series numbers.

> COMPETITION CARS NOT FOR PUBLIC SALE
> **R.L. TARGA FLORIO 1923 -** OPEN TOP RACER
> **20-30 E.S. SPORT** WITH G1 ENGINE (SPECIAL ELABORATION BY MEROSI BASED ON INFORMATION PROVIDED BY ENZO FERRARI)
> **G.P.R.** (GRAND PRIX ROMEO) ALSO DESCRIBED AS P1. TWO-SEATER GRAND PRIX CAR.

1924

R.M. SPORT

4 cylinders in line, 1996 cc, 44 hp, single camshaft in crankcase. Wheelbase 2900 mm.

Chassis for:

TOURER. SALOON, ROADSTER,…

Technical characteristics very similar to those of the Normale, except for a slight increase in cubic capacity and a relative power increase of 4 hp.

"Superflex" beaded tyres 800x130.
Chassis and engines included in R.L. Normale numbers for 1923.

Torpedo Sport (con capotta incassata) su chassis R. M. Sport

Sports tourer (with hood down) on an R.M. Sport chassis.

NO SIGNIFICANT MODIFICATIONS TO THE FOLLOWING MODELS:

R.M. Normale. Chassis and engine numbers not available.
R.L. Normale (4th Series). Chassis and engines from 7851 to 8404.
R.L. Sport (4th Series). Chassis and engines included in Normale numbers.
R.L. Normale (5th Series). Chassis and engines from 8351 to 8404.
R.L. Sport (5th Series). Chassis and engines included in Normale numbers.

COMPETITION CARS NOT FOR PUBLIC SALE
R.L. TARGA FLORIO 1924 - TWO-SEATER SPORT
P2 - TWO-SEATER GRAND PRIX CAR (CONCEIVED BY VITTORIO JANO)

1925

RM UNIFICATO

4 cylinders in line, 1996 cc, 48 hp, single camshaft in crankcase. Wheelbase 3220 mm.

Chassis for:

TOURER, SALOON,
ROADSTER,...

Apart from the longer wheelbase to accommodate bigger bodies, the new chassis did not differ from the Normale or Sport.
"Superflex" beaded tyres 775x145.
Chassis and engines from 13001 to 13278.

R.L. SUPER SPORT (6th SERIES)

6 cylinders in line, 2994 cc, 83 hp, single camshaft in crankcase. Wheelbase 3140 mm.

Chassis for:

TOURER, LIMOUSINE,
ROADSTER,...

The Supersport had two Zenith carburettors (below) and the classical dihedral radiator, which had already appeared on some Sport models. It also had a new dry sump lubrication system, which improved both the lubrication and oil cooling.
"Superflex Cord" beaded tyres 820x120 with spoked wheels.
Chassis and engines from 069001 to 069291

> **NO SIGNIFICANT MODIFICATIONS TO THE FOLLOWING MODEL:**
> **R.L. Normale (5th Series).** Chassis and engines from 8405 to 8850.

1926

R.L. TURISMO (6th SERIES)

6 cylinders in line, 2994 cc, 61 hp, single camshaft in crankcase. Wheelbase 3443 mm.

Chassis for:

TOURER, LIMOUSINE,
ROADSTER,...

The name of the **R.L. Normale** was changed to Turismo and the cubic capacity was brought into line with the Super Sport with a power increase of 5 hp.
Beaded tyres 860x160 with spoked wheels.
Chassis and engines from 069301 to 069500.

R.L. TURISMO (7th SERIES)

6 cylinders in line, 2994 cc, 61 hp, single camshaft in crankcase. Wheelbase 3443 mm.

Chassis for:

TOURER, LIMOUSINE,
ROADSTER,...

No significant modifications, except for an increase in the diameter of the front and rear brake drums from 360 mm to 420mm.
Chassis and engines from 069501 to 069700.

R.L. SUPER SPORT (7th SERIES)

6 cylinders in line, 2994 cc, 83 hp, single camshaft in crankcase. Wheelbase 3140 mm.

Chassis for:

TOURER, LIMOUSINE,
ROADSTER,...

Production continued without particular variations, except for the increased diameter of the brake drums in common with the Turismo model.
Chassis and engines from 069292 to 069300.

NO SIGNIFICANT MODIFICATIONS TO THE FOLLOWING MODEL:
RM Unificato. Chassis and engines included in 1925 numbers.

6C 1500 NORMALE (1st SERIES)

6 cylinders in line, 1487 cc, 44 hp, single overhead camshaft.
Wheelbase 2900 mm or 3100 mm for six-seater bodies.

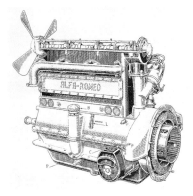

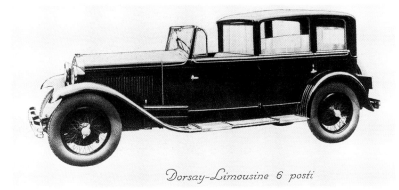

Dorsay-Limousine 6 posti

Chassis for:

TOURER, SALOON, ROADSTER,...

The 6C 1500 represented a radical change of direction for Alfa Romeo, brought about by Vittorio Jano. It was logical that all projects should benefit from experience gained during the construction of the **P2** in as much that the development of the new car found a point of equilibrium between high power, low chassis weight, handling and stability.

The six cylinder in line engine with a single overhead camshaft was a single fusion in cast iron which provided for cylinder groups and head, while the sump and the crankcase, which contained the drive shaft, were made of aluminium. The first group of engines had small sumps. The petrol tank was located behind the dashboard.

The long chassis was fitted with *Straight Side* wheels (1) 20 inches in diameter with a 4" channel, while the short chassis's rims were 19 inches in diameter with the same 4" channel.

Tyres "Superflex Cord" 30"x5.25" or 29"x5.25".

Chassis and engines from 0110751 to 0111250.

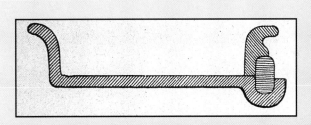

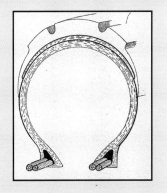

(1) The *Straight Side* system (straight bead) had been used in America for some time when it reached Italy. It held the tyre in the rim by means of a metal ring fixed to the wheel itself. The size 28x4.95 was the equivalent of 5.00"x19", while the 30"x5.25" could be substituted by the 5.25"x20". New tyres were under development which would also be adopted for subsequent semi-channel rims, conceptually similar to those still in use today.

NO SIGNIFICANT MODIFICATIONS TO THE FOLLOWING MODELS
R.L. Turismo (7th Series). Chassis and engines from 069501 to 069700 (including those of 1926).
R.L. Super Sport (7th Series). Chassis and engines from 069701 to 069850 (including those of 1926).

6C 1500 NORMALE (2nd SERIES)

6 cylinders in line, 1487 cc, 44 hp, single overhead camshaft. Wheelbase 2900 mm.
Or 3100 mm for 6 seater bodies.

Chassis for:

TOURER, SALOON,
ROADSTER,…

The modifications to in the 2nd series, the date of the introduction of which could not be established, included a larger sump and a slightly bigger oil filter; the gearbox was also revised with the substitution of the sliding reverse gear and the direct drive shaft; the rear brake lever was also modified; in addition, the differential driving worm of the steering box was changed.

The body was given new rear leaf springs, new supports for the running boards which were different for the long and short wheelbase models; specific protection for the thrust tube on the floor. The petrol tank was also modified.
The 2nd series was fitted with a 19 inch diameter wheel with 4" channel and tyres size 29"x5.25".
The production of this model is believed to have ended in 1928, although it is possible some were al-

Weymann saloon, Farina factory.

so made in 1929.
Chassis and engines from 0111501 to 0111800.

6C 1500 SPORT (2nd SERIES)

6 cylinders in line, 1487 cc, 54 hp, twin overhead camshafts. Wheelbase 2920 mm.

Chassis for:

SALOON, ROADSTER

This was the first Alfa Romeo to be sold to the public with twin overhead camshafts and the head in cast iron, innovations which were, at that time, used only for the racing cars. A trait which, more than any other, characterises the Portello company and was not abandoned even if, for some time to come, the single overhead camshaft was used

for the **6C 1500 Normale** and **6C 1750 Touring** models. To reduce noise and provide inertia to the more complex distribution system, the front extremities of the camshafts were given two pulleys which functioned as flywheels with a third anchored in the head, which also worked as a flywheel.
The engine had a bigger sump, already used for the 2nd series Normale model. The petrol tank was located at the rear.
The short wheelbase enabled body builders to produce roadsters with sporting overtones. Even if the wheelbase apparently rendered the chassis identical to that of the short Normale (2900 mm), longitudinal members were similar, but the cross members were of different design. In addition, the Sport chassis was different in other ways: length of the front leaf springs 720 mm and the rears 1070 mm; distance of the

rear wheel centre to the attachment of the rear spring 520 mm.
Tyres "Superflex Cord" 28"x5.25" with Straight Side wheels; possible substitution with tyres in size 4.75"x18" and 5.25"x18" (see 1927 note). It appears that this model was only produced in 1928, but it is possible production was continued in 1929.
Chassis and engines from 0211313 to 0211400, from 0211413 to 0211505.

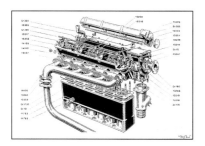

Garavini roadster.

6C 1500 MILLE MIGLIA SPECIALE (2nd SERIES)

6 cylinders in line, 1487 cc, 60 hp (76 hp with supercharger),
twin overhead camshafts. Wheelbase 2920 mm.

Engine seen from the front.

Engine from the induction side.

Chassis for:

ROADSTER

Only 24 of these cars were made and 12 were built in a year. A Roots-type supercharger with a rotation ratio of 1.4:1 in relation to the engine was fitted to some cars. The engine was dropped back 20 cm and the petrol tank was placed in the rear above the chassis. Sometimes, these cars were erroneously called the **6C 1500 Super Sport**, but that is the name of the **6C 1750 Super Sport** which was produced in 1929 with an engine of reduced cubic capacity so that it could compete in the racing class of up to 1500 cc. The engines were characterised by the three external pulleys. The radiator was vertical. Tyres "Superflex Cord" 27"x4.75" with *Straight Side* wheels of 18"x4". That size corresponds to 4.75"x18". **Chassis and engines from 0211301 to 0211312.**

The chassis.

6C 1750 TURISMO (3ʳᵈ SERIES)

6 cylinders in line, 1752 cc, 46 hp, single overhead camshaft. Wheelbase 3100 mm.

Chassis for:

TOURER, SALOON, ROADSTER,…

The 6C began its evolution and the cubic capacity neared two litres. This chassis was suitable not only for the closed bodies of saloons, but also had Tourer and Roadster bodies.

The chassis was slightly modified compared to the **6C 1500 Normale** with a 3100 mm wheelbase. In respect of the 2ⁿᵈ Series, the engine went through a profound transformation: the head, still in cast iron, could be taken off the cylinder group, which eased maintenance; the plugs were located on the left side of the head, while the induc-

Torpedo 4 posti, con baule

Four seater Tourer with boot

tion manifold and exhaust were placed on the right.

Tyres "Superflex Cord" 29"x5.25" (equivalent to 5.25"x19"), wheels 19 inch *Straight Side* with a 4"

channel.
Chassis and engines from 0411851 to 0412179.

6C 1750 SPORT (3ʳᵈ SERIES)

6 cylinders in line, 1752 cc, 52 hp, twin overhead camshafts. Wheelbase 2920 mm.

Chassis for:

TOURER, SALOON, ROADSTER,…

The cubic capacity of the Sport model was also increased. The engine characteristics did not vary greatly from the previous **6C 1500 Sport**, except that the new exhaust manifold was fitted with a finned cooling device. The new balanced gears meant the elimination of the three external pulleys used for the previous system.

The wheels were *Straight Side* up until the 129ᵗʰ car, after which channelled wheels in the same 18"x4" size were introduced.

The remaining characteristics of the chassis were unchanged. It is believed that this car was only produced in 1929 but the possibility of

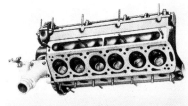

Touring cabriolet.

it being continued in 1930 cannot be ruled out.

Chassis and engines from 0212506 to 0212783.

6C 1750 SUPER SPORT (3rd SERIES)

6 cylinders in line, 1752 cc, 64 hp (85 hp with supercharger), twin overhead camshafts. Wheelbase 2750 mm.

Chassis for:

TOURER, ROADSTER,...

The principal difference with this model was the shortening of the wheelbase; the new supercharged version was built in a manner not very dissimilar to the **6C 1500 Mille Miglia Speciale.** It was, in fact, available with or without a supercharger (still with a fast rotation ratio: 1.4:1 in relation to the engine

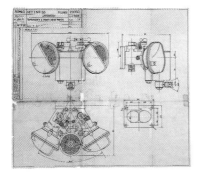

fitted with the new Memini DOA horizontal twin choke carburettor in place of the Zenith 42 HA shown in the drawing on the left) and also with 1487 cubic capacity, none of which makes it easy to identify the different models.
Unsupercharged cars had a extension of the front support cover of the engine, which also contained the starting handle shaft. The sump of the supercharged version was slightly increased in size.
The petrol tank, placed above the chassis behind the seat, was cylinder-shaped. Fuel supply was by Nivex. A supplementary oil tank was used and placed on the left, behind the dashboard, which facilitated the topping up of the sump by opening a tap. Conic torque for the supercharged version: 12x49, 13x49, 13x51; unsupercharged

Zagato roadster.

11x51, 12x51, 12x54.
The radiator of the **6C 1750 Super Sport** was inclined and lowered.
Tyres "Superflex Cord" 27"x4.75" with *Straight Side* wheels. The size was the equivalent of 4.75"x18".
It is believed this model was only produced in 1929, but continuation of manufacture in 1930 cannot be excluded.
Chassis and engines from 0312851 to 0312971.

6C 1500 SUPER SPORT (3rd SERIES)

6 cylinders in line, 1487 cc, 60 hp (76 hp with supercharger), twin overhead camshafts. Wheelbase 2750 mm.

Chassis for:

TOURER, ROADSTER,...

Sold with or without supercharger (photographs) the car's characteristics were identical to those of the **6C 1750 Super Sport**, but with a cubic capacity reduced to one-and-a-half litres for participation in the 1500 cc class of racing's' Sport category.
It could seem just a simple engine modification but since these cars, built by Alfa Romeo, took part in

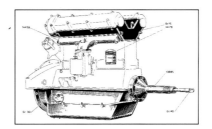

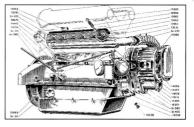

competition as did the **6C 1500 Super Sport** it is correct to consider them specific models.
Chassis and engines included in 6C 1750 Super Sport numbers.

NO SIGNIFICANT MODIFICATIONS TO THE FOLLOWING MODEL:
6C 1500 Mille Miglia Speciale (2nd Series). Chassis and engines from 0211401 to 0211412.

6C 1750 TURISMO (3rd SERIES)

6 cylinders in line, 1752 cc, 46 hp, single overhead camshaft. Wheelbase 3100 mm.

Chassis for:

TOURER, SALOON,
ROADSTER,...

Few mechanical variations, with the exception of the diameter of the main journal connecting rod of the camshaft which, from engine number 0412201, passed from the original 46 mm and 40 mm of the 6C 1500 to 48 mm and 42 mm respectively. The induction manifold and carburettor underwent slight modifications and some corrections were made to the box of the rear axle and brake drums. More reliable springs were fitted.
This was the first model with its body built by Alfa Romeo. It seems production of the 3rd Series Tourer ended in 1930, but it may have continued in 1931. **Chassis and engines from 0412180 to 0412448.**

6C 1750 GRAN TURISMO (4th SERIES)

6 cylinders in line, 1752 cc, 55 hp, twin overhead camshafts. Wheelbase 2920 mm.

Chassis for:

SALOON, ROADSTER,
CABRIOLET, FAUX
CABRIOLET, TOURER,...

The **6C 1750 Sport** 3rd Series gave way to the Gran Turismo. The general lay-out remained unchanged: wheelbase, track and mechanical characteristics, while power was increased by 3 hp. Journal and toe pins measured respectively 42 mm and 48 mm.
Tyres 28"x5.50" with 18"x4" *Straight Side* wheels until car number 8613329; after that, channelled wheels.
It seems the 4th Series was only produced in 1930, but continuation in 1931 cannot be excluded. **Chassis and engines from 8613201 to 8613600.**

Semi-rigid saloon.

Faux cabriolet.

6C 1750 GRAN SPORT (4th SERIES)

6 cylinders in line, 1752 cc, 85 hp, twin overhead camshafts, supercharged.
Wheelbase 2745 mm.

Chassis for:

ROADSTER, COUPE',
CABRIOLET,...

A new design, bigger volumetric supercharger but with a rotation ratio of 1:1 in relation to the engine, therefore slower than that fitted to the **6C 1750 Super Sport**, distinguished the new car. The carburettor was a twin-choke Memini. The wheelbase was reduced because different spring attachments were used measuring 720mm front and

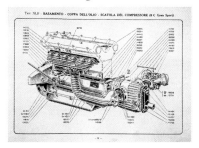

940 mm rear; the distance from the wheel centre to the rear spring attachment measured 525 mm instead of 520 mm of the **6C 1750 Super Sport** and **6C 1750 Gran Turismo**; the chassis cross members changed while the lateral longitudinal members remained identical, the height of the central area of which was 110 mm, while the chassis of the **6C 1750 Turismo** measured 120 mm. As with the Super Sport, the width of the rear of the chassis was 960 mm. Conic torque of the differential: 12x49, 12x51, 12x54, 13x51. The shape of the petrol tank was changed from cylindrical to oval and it was placed at the rear near the spare wheel. An O.S. fuel system took the place of the Le Nivex.

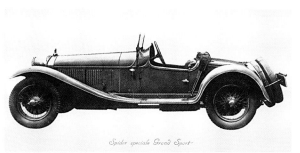

Spider speciale Grand Sport.

The colour of the instrument dials was changed from white to black. Tyres 5.00"/5.25"x18" with 18"x4" channelled wheels.
Production of the Gran Sport 4th Series is believed to have been in 1930 only, but continuation in 1931 cannot be excluded.
Chassis and engines from 8513001 to 8513100.

6C 1500 GRAN SPORT (4th SERIES)

6 cylinders in line, 1487 cc, 80 hp, twin overhead camshafts, supercharged.
Wheelbase 2745 mm.

Chassis for:

ROADSTER, COUPE',
CABRIOLET,...

As happened with the **6C 1500 Super Sport**, the cubic capacity of some examples of the **6C 1750 Gran Sport** was reduced to 1500 cc so that they could race in that class. No other modification was carried out.
Like the **6C 1500 Super Sport**, mention of these cars is essential because they were officially called **6C 1500 Gran Sport** by the company.
Chassis and engines included in 6C

1750 Gran Sport numbers.

COMPETITION CARS NOT FOR PUBLIC SALE
6C 1750 GRAN SPORT TESTA FISSA - RACING ROADSTER
P2/1930 - RACING ROADSTER
(THREE EXAMPLES RESULTING FROM THE ELABORATION OF THE 1924 MODEL)

6C 1750 TURISMO (4ᵗʰ SERIES)

6 cylinders in line, 1752 cc, 46 hp, single overhead camshaft. Wheelbase 3100 mm.

Chassis for:

TOURER, SALOON,
ROADSTER,...

The "Mignon" model, with a body by Touring.

Compared to the **6C 1750 Turismo** (3ʳᵈ Series), the width of the rear of the chassis went from 960 mm to 1040 mm and the distance from the centres of the rear springs from 920 mm to 1000 mm. Spring length was changed from 760 mm to 720 mm front and 1170 mm to 1050 mm rear. The front shock absorbers were fitted outside the chassis, the rear ends of which were joined by a bar which served as the spare wheel support. The rear cross member near the axle cradle was laid out differently. Outside were more modern attachments for the boot, which were previously more or less those of the **6C 1500 Normale,** with an outside hook fixed to the chassis and small handles on each side with which to lift the boot. The feed manifold was modified again. There were a few more small variations, including 5.50"/6.00"x18" tyres on 18"x4.50" wheels. **Chassis and engines from 8713701 to 8713776.**

6C 1750 GRAN TURISMO (5ᵗʰ SERIES)

6 cylinders in line, 1752 cc, 55 hp, twin overhead camshafts. Wheelbase 2920 mm.

Chassis for:

SALOON, ROADSTER,
FAUX, CABRIOLET,
TOURER,...

A modification was introduced to accommodate the camshaft drive, which formed a single body with the cast iron cylinder group. A bigger clutch was fitted.
Tyres 5.50"x18" with channelled wheels size 18"x4". **Chassis and engines from 10914401 to 10914660.**

6C 1750 GRAN SPORT (5ᵗʰ SERIES)

6 cylinders in line, 1752 cc, 85 hp, twin overhead camshafts, supercharger. Wheelbase 2745 mm.

Chassis for:

ROADSTER, COUPE',
CABRIOLET,...

The modification to accommodate the camshaft drive was also made to the Gran Sport by being incorporated to form a single unit with the cast iron cylinder group, plus all other mechanical changes which were made to the base model. The two new cylinder retaining studs, placed in the cylinder group, required a modification to the cylinder head. From the 61ˢᵗ car onwards, the petrol tank was modified by the addition of a petrol tank level indicator made by Azimut. Chassis and spring sizes identical to those of the 4ᵗʰ Series. Two fuel feeders were added and new clutch discs were introduced. No other significant modification. **Chassis and engines from 10814301 to 10814376.**

6C 1500 GRAN SPORT (5th SERIES)

6 cylinders in line, 1487 cc, 80 hp, twin overhead camshafts, supercharger.
Wheelbase 2745 mm.

Chassis for:

ROADSTER, COUPE',
CABRIOLET,...

As with the **6C 1750 Gran Sport** 4th Series, the cubic capacity of some of the 5th Series production was reduced so that they could race in the up to 1500 cc class.
Chassis and engines included in 6C 1750 Gran Sport numbers.

Zagato Roadster.

6C 1750 GRAN TURISMO
COMPRESSORE (5th SERIES)

6 cylinders in line, 1752 cc, 80 hp, twin overhead camshafts, supercharger.
Wheelbase 3160 mm.

Marinoni and Cortese aboard the Touring saloon.

Chassis for:

SALOON, COUPE',
ROADSTER,
CABRIOLET,...

Compared to the sporting versions of the 6C, the GTC was distinguished by a longer, wider chassis as a result of the bigger track (1420 mm), thanks to springs located outside the chassis. The car was produced for customers who wanted high performance combined with maximum driving comfort. Body weight penalised the car's performance, however; Carrozzeria Touring built very light saloons at that time (picture), one of which won the 2000cc Saloon Class of the 1932 Mille Miglia, driven by Nando Minoia.

In line with the 5th Series modifications, the camshaft drive system was incorporated in the cylinder block, instead of being separate, as in other twin overhead camshaft versions; the clutch size was increased.
The volumetric supercharger, identical to that of the **6C 1750 Gran Sport,** was fitted with a new type of twin-choke Memini carburettor.
This was the only model in the 6C Series (up until the 7th) in which there was a reduced distance between the steering wheel and the steering box which went from 1082 mm to 1076 mm. The length of the rear springs was 1010 mm.
Tyres 30x6 with channelled wheels of 18"x4.50". The size is equivalent to 6.00"x18".
Chassis and engines from 101014801 to 101014861.

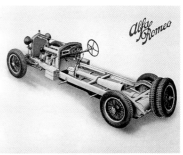

The chassis.

8C 2300 (1ˢᵗ SERIES)

8 cylinders in line, 2336 cc, 142 hp, twin overhead camshafts, supercharger.
Wheelbase 2750 mm and 3100 mm.

Car chassis for:

SALOON, ROADSTER,
CABRIOLET,…

A masterpiece by Vittorio Jano, the **8C 2300** was a marvellous eight cylinder with twin overhead camshafts and volumetric super-

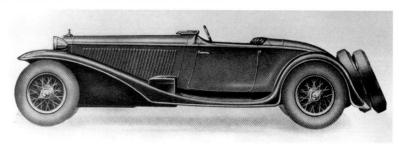

charger.
Two types of chassis for different purposes: one for competition (short chassis) and the other to support the elegant bodies of either the cabriolet or saloon for use as touring cars (long chassis). Width of the front of the chassis 640 mm, rear 920 mm.
Length of front springs 760 mm, rear 940 mm.
Chassis and engines from 2111001 to 2111024.

The Zagato roadster.

Exhaust side of the engine.

Induction side of the engine.

COMPETITION CAR NOT FOR PUBLIC SALE
A TYPE – A GRAND PRIX SINGLE SEATER

1932

_ 6C 1750 GRAN TURISMO (5th SERIES) _

6 cylinders in line, 1752 cc, 55 hp, twin overhead camshafts. Wheelbase 2920 mm.

Chassis for:

SALOON, ROADSTER,
FAUX, CABRIOLET,
TOURER,...

Production continued without significant changes. The gearbox was modified with a different breather device for oil vapour.
Chassis and engines from 10914661 to 10914726.

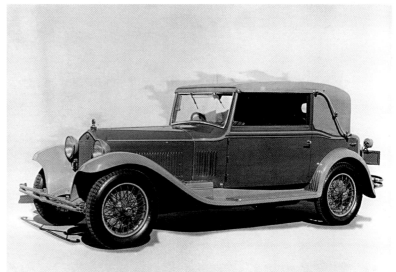

Cabriolet Castagna.

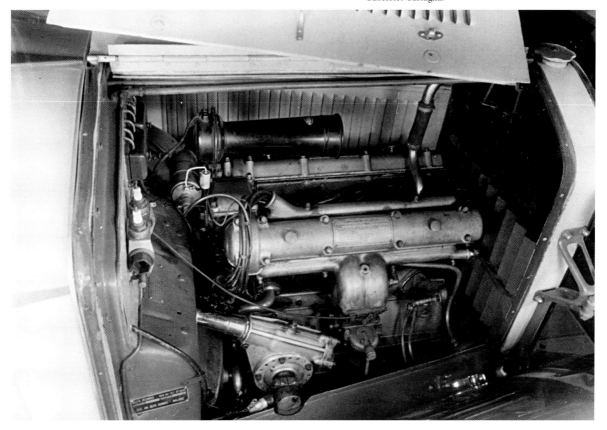

31

1932

8C 2300 (2nd SERIES)

8 cylinders in line, 2336 cc, 142 hp, twin overhead camshafts, supercharger.
Wheelbase 2750 mm and 3100 mm.

8c Long Type
TWO-SEATER COUPE'
with ample boot space

8c Long model
ROYAL CABRIOLET
Two-seater with ample
Boot space and a third casual seat

Chassis for:

SALOON, ROADSTER,
CABRIOLET,...

Modifications to the **8C 2300** introduced with the 2nd series were: front spring length reduced to 740 mm from the 750 mm of the 1st series; inclination of the steering wheel was reduced by 40 mm on the long wheelbase version; the length of the steering column was reduced to 1036 mm from 1040 mm on the short wheelbase model. From the 28th car, the electric fuel pump was placed in the rear of the car, close to the fuel tank on the short wheelbase model.
Numerous bodies were produced by the best builders, in particular Zagato and Touring. They included sports type bodies, elegant roadsters, coupès and sports saloons. **Chassis and engines from 2211051 to 2211092.**

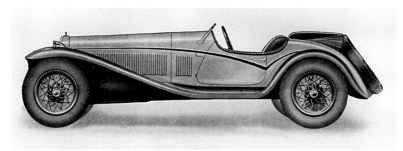

Touring Roadster

NO SIGNIFICANT MODIFICATIONS TO THE FOLLOWING MODELS:
6C 1750 Turismo (4th Series). Chassis and engines from 8713777 to 8714124.
6C 1750 Gran Sport (5th Series). Chassis and engine numbers from 10814377 to 10814406.
6C 1500 Gran Sport (5th Series). Chassis and engine numbers included in those of the **6C 1750 Gran Sport.**
6C 1750 Gran Turismo Supercharged (5th Series). Chassis and engines from 101014862 to 101014962.
8C 2300 (1st Series). Chassis and engines from 101014862 to 101014962.

COMPETITION CAR NOT FOR PUBLIC SALE
TYPE B (P3) - GRAND PRIX SINGLE SEATER

1933

—— 6C 1750 GRAN SPORT (6th SERIES) ——

6 cylinders in line, 1752 cc, 85 hp, twin overhead camshafts, supercharger. Wheelbase 2745 mm.

Chassis for:

ROADSTER, COUPE',
CABRIOLET,...

While retracing the imposition of the previous models, the sixth series G.S. included all the updates, which were introduced on the 6C 1900 at the same time: box-type chassis, but still characterised by longitudinal chassis members 110 mm wide in the central area, free wheel, bigger radiator and a gear-box with synchronised third gear. The inclination of the steering wheel was reduced by 5 mm (the inner rim of the wheel was 345 mm from the chassis base). The clutch was made smaller.

Tyres 5.25"/5.50"x18" with channelled wheels. It appears that the production of the 6th Series of the Gran Sport took place in 1933, but the possibility of it having continued in 1934 cannot be excluded. **Chassis and engines from 121215031 to 121215071.**

Zagato Roadster

_ 6C 1900 GRAN TURISMO (6th SERIES) _

6 cylinders in line, 1917 cc, 68 hp, twin overhead camshafts. Wheelbase 2925 mm.

ALFA ROMEO SALOON
AND CHASSIS FOR
ROADSTER, CABRIOLET,...

With the 6C 1900, the aluminium cylinder head was introduced and replaced cast iron, which had been used for all cars produced by the company up until that point.
The **6C 1900 GT** included numer-ous innovations: box-type chassis welded instead of riveted in some areas to increase rigidity, a gearbox with free wheel capability (photo above), a bigger capacity water radiator and a synchronised third gear. Front and rear track measurements went from the usual 1380 mm to 1420 mm, therefore assuming the same size as the **6C 1750 GTC** of 1931; the length of the front springs increased by 20 mm to become 740 mm.
Tyres 5.50"x18" with channelled wheel size 18"x4". Veglia instruments.
It appears production of the 6th Series of the GT took place in 1933 only, but its continuation in 1934 cannot be ruled out. **Chassis and engines from 121315101 o 121315300.**

———— 8C 2300 (3rd SERIES) ————

8 cylinders in line, 2336 cc, 142 hp, twin overhead camshafts, supercharger.
Wheelbase 2750 mm and 3100 mm.

Chassis for:

SALOON, ROADSTER,
CABRIOLET,...

In 1933 a new, less capacious oval oil tank was introduced as was a new exhaust system. Minor modifications were also made to the front axle.

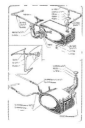

Chassis and engine numbers from   2311201 to 2311243.

> **NO SIGNIFICANT MODIFICATIONS WERE MADE TO THE FOLLOWING MODELS:**
> **6C 1750 Turismo (4th Series).** Chassis and engines from 8714125 to 8714202.
> **8C 2300 (2nd Series).** Chassis and engines from 2211093 to 2211139.

> COMPETITION CAR NOT FOR PUBLIC SALE
> **8C 2600 MONZA** - TWO-SEATER FOR GRANDS PRIX AND ROAD RACING

6C 2300 TURISMO (7th SERIES)

6 cylinders in line, 2309 cc, 68 hp, twin overhead camshafts. Wheelbase 3213 mm.

ALFA ROMEO SALOON AND CHASSIS FOR COUPE',...

First exhibited at the Milan Motor Show in April, 1934, this new car was an evolution of the 6C 1900. Called the 7th Series and, therefore, a descendent of the **6C 1500 Normale** which first appeared in 1927, the car was a transition model which led to the 6C 2300 B, first of a long series of models the production of which was due to continue with the 6C 2500 and conclude in 1953. From 1934, superchargers were no longer fitted to 6C models but the aluminium head with twin overhead camshafts was also used for Turismo cars. The drive was no longer by gears but through silent chains, a system which Alfa Romeo retained unaltered for a long time. The design of the engine, therefore, was a complete evolution of the previous 6C 1900. The fuel pump became electric, the clutch a dry mono-disc with

flexible coupling springs. Like the **6C 1750 GTC** and the **6C 1900 GT**, the springs were outside the chassis, the ends of which were connected by a bar to increase rigidity. The shock absorbers were friction-type and the brakes mechanical. Tyres 6.00"x18" with channelled wheels. Veglia instruments. **Chassis and engines from 710501 a to 710722.**

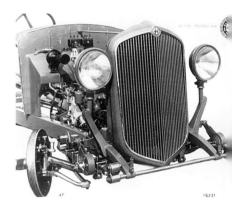

The six-seater saloon with standard body.

6C 2300 GRAN TURISMO (7th SERIES)

6 cylinders in line, 2309 cc, 76 hp, twin overhead camshafts. Wheelbase 2925 mm.

ALFA ROMEO SALOON AND CHASSIS FOR: COUPE', CABRIOLET, ROADSTER,...

With a shorter wheelbase which only in size reflects those of the 1500 Sport and the 1750 Gran Turismo, came the sportier version of the 6C 2300. The engine, naturally, had twin overhead camshafts driven by silent chains. Higher performance was achieved by a different compression ratio and drive shafts in common with the Sport model. Electric fuel pump. Extremely equilibrated and elegant, the aerody-

The production saloon with body by Alfa Romeo.

namic saloon body was built by Alfa Romeo itself. Tyres 5.50"x18" with channelled

wheels. **Chassis and engines from 700101 to 700635.**

6C 2300 PESCARA
(6C 2300 SPORT)* (7ᵗʰ SERIES)

6 cylinders in line, 2309 cc, 95 hp, twin overhead camshafts. Wheelbase 2925 mm.

Chassis for:

SALOON, TOURER, CABRIOLET, COUPE',...

Only 60 examples were made. The Pescara retained the chassis characteristics of the **6C 2300 Gran Turismo**, but it was a high performance car able to excel in road racing due to a higher compression cylinder head with a third spring for each valve and twin carburettors which ensured better fuel feed. The drive shafts were the same as those of the GT. The exhaust was also improved with a different box.

The fuel tank was completely redesigned for greater capacity, with the consequent modification of the spare wheel support. Rear springs were also modified. Axle ratio 12/51.

Tyres 5.50"x18" with channelled wheels.

Chassis and engine numbers included in those of the 6C 2300 Gran Turismo.

Above and below: the Touring saloons

*This definition, used in both the spare parts catalogue and other official publications, suggests it was the true denomination established by Alfa. Yet the echo of the victory at Pescara in the 1934 Targa Abruzzo predominated and the company evidently decided to conform.

NO SIGNIFICANT MODIFICATIONS TO THE FOLLOWING MODEL:
8C 2300 (3ᴿᴰ SERIES). Chassis and engine numbers from 2311244 to 2311250.

COMPETITION CAR NOT FOR PUBLIC SALE
1934 TYPE B - GRAND PRIX SINGLE-SEATER

_ 6C 2300 B GRAN TURISMO (1st SERIES) _

6 cylinders in line, 2309 cc, 76 hp, twin overhead camshafts. Wheelbase 3000 mm.

ALFA ROMEO SALOON
AND
CHASSIS FOR
CABRIOLET,…

The 6C 2300 B was a completely new project which was to be further developed with the 6C 2500 in 1939. While retaining the twin overhead camshaft engines of the previous 6C 2300, it had a modern chassis with independent front and rear wheels, rear axle suspended elastically from the chassis and hydraulic brakes instead of the mechanical units fitted to Alfas until the appearance of this model. To sanction this major step forward in quality, the sequence of the series, initiated in 1927 with the **6C 1500 Normale**, was discontinued.

The saloons were built entirely by Alfa Romeo while the cabriolet and coupè versions were constructed by outside body builders. Tyres 5.50x18 with spoked wheels. **Chassis from 813001 to 813015; included between the numbers 823001 to 823184.**

The Alfa Romeo-built saloon.

____ 6C 2300 B PESCARA (1st SERIES) ____

6 cylinders in line, 2309 cc, 95 hp, twin overhead camshafts. Wheelbase 3000 mm.

Cabriolet Castagna.

Chassis for:

SPORTS SALOON, CABRIOLET,…

The modification of four independent wheels was also extended to the Pescara, which retained the high performance engine of the previous 6C 2300 7th Series. Only four of these cars were built. Tyres 5.50"x18" with spoked wheels. **Chassis and engine numbers from 813801 to 813804.**

Pinin Farina coupè

COMPETITION CARS NOT FOR PUBLIC SALE
TYPE B 1935 - SINGLE-SEATER GRAND PRIX CAR
BIMOTORE (TWIN ENGINE) GRAND PRIX SINGLE-SEATER
8C 1935 - GRAND PRIX SINGLE-SEATER
8C 2900 A - TWO-SEATER RACER

1936

—— 6C 2300 B TURISMO (1st SERIES) ——

6 cylinders in line, 2309 cc, 70 hp, twin overhead camshafts. Wheelbase 3250 mm.

ALFA ROMEO SIX SEATER SALOON

Large and imposing saloon for prestige use. Only two examples produced during the year.
Tyres 6.00"x18" with channelled wheels.
Chassis and engine numbers from 814001 to 814002.

Berlina Alfa Romeo/Castagna.

NO SIGNIFICANT MODIFICATIONS TO THE FOLLOWING MODELS:
6C 2300 B Gran Turismo (1st Series). Chassis from 813016 to 813019; engines from 823001 to 823184.
6C 2300 B Pescara (1st Series). Chassis and engine numbers from 813805 to 813809.

COMPETITION CAR NOT FOR PUBLIC SALE
8C 2900 A - TWO-SEATER RACING ROADSTER - **12C 1936** - GRAND PRIX SINGLE-SEATER

1937

8C 2900 B

8 cylinders in line, 2905 cc, 180 hp, twin overhead camshafts, twin superchargers.
Wheelbase 2800 mm and 3000 mm.

Chassis for:

ROADSTER, COUPE',
SPORTS SALOON,...

An insuperable car built with the **Tipo B 1935** Grand Prix racing car engine with a slightly reduced cubic capacity which, two years earlier, was fitted to the **8C 2900 A** Spider Corsa of which three examples were built and which dominated the 1936 Mille Miglia.

The 8C 2900 B had two volumetric superchargers, the cylinder grouping in light alloy was divided between two blocks each of four cylinders with cylinder sleeves of driven steel.

The possibility of having either long or short chassis gave outside body builders ample flexibility.

A reduction of 40 cc compared to the **8C 2900 A** made the car accessible to a larger clientele, all of whom had to possess notable driving skills.

Tyres 5.50"x19" on spoked wheels.
Chassis numbers from 412011 to 412020; engines from 422011 to 422020.

The engine and chassis.

Two sports saloons by Touring.

NO SIGNIFICANT MODIFICATIONS TO THE FOLLOWING MODELS:

6C 2300 B Turismo (1ˢᵗ Series). Chassis from 814003 to 814081; engines from 823001 to 823184.
6C 2300 B Gran Turismo (1ˢᵗ Series). Chassis from 813020 to 813098; engines from 823001 to 823184.
6C 2300 B Pescara (1ˢᵗ Series). Chassis and engines from 813810 to 813915.

COMPETITION CAR NOT FOR PUBLIC SALE
12C 1937 - GRAND PRIX SINGLE-SEATER

1938

6C 2300 B CORTO (2nd SERIES)

6 cylinders in line, 2309 cc, 76 hp, twin overhead camshafts. Wheelbase 3000 mm.

ALFA ROMEO FOUR SEATER SALOON AND CHASSIS FOR CABRIOLET,...

The 2nd Series incorporated several modifications, among them the substitution of the electric fuel pump for a mechanical unit housed on the engine, a new gearbox with syn-chronised 3rd and 4th gears and silent gear mechanisms always in motion for 2nd, 3rd and 4th. The transmission was fitted with elastic joints and the spherical bearings of the differential were substituted by taper roller bearings.
Tyres 6.00"x18" with artillery wheels.

Chassis from 813201 to 813398; engines from 823185 to 823650.

Pinin Farina Cabriolet

6C 2300 B LUNGO (2nd SERIES)

6 cylinders in line, 2309 cc, 70 hp, twin overhead camshafts. Wheelbase 3250 mm.

ALFA ROMEO SALOON 6-7 SEATS AND CHASSIS FOR SALOON, CABRIOLET, COUPE',...

The chassis of the short **6C 2300 B Corto** made longer and with a slightly less powerful engine.
Chassis from 814101 to 814316; engine from 823185 to 823650.

Pinin Farina Saloon

6C 2300 B MILLE MIGLIA (2nd SERIE)

6 cylinders in line, 2309 cc, 95 hp, twin overhead camshafts. Wheelbase 3000 mm.

Chassis for:

SPORTS TOURER WITH 4 SEATS

This car takes its name from the sporting saloon Alfa Romeo prepared for the 1937 Mille Miglia, but with a new and lighter body by Carrozzeria Touring. The car came fourth driven by Alfa test driver Giovanbattista Guidotti, whose co-driver for publicity reasons was Mussolini's chauffeur, Ercole Boratto. To mark that success, Alfa built a small series of the car for public sale with a 10 hp reduction in engine power. Tyres 5.50"x18" with spoked wheels.
Chassis from 815001 to 815101; engine from 823916 to 823968; from 824001 to 824051.

Sports Tourer by Touring

NO SIGNIFICANT MODIFICATIONS TO THE FOLLOWING MODELS:
6C 2300 B Gran Turismo (1st Series). Chassis from 813099 to 813103; engines from 823001 to 823184.
8C 2900 B. Chassis from 412021 to 412042; engines from 422021 to 422042.

COMPETITION CARS NOT FOR PUBLIC SALE
312 – 308 – 158 – 316
GRAND PRIX SINGLE-SEATERS

6C 2500 TURISMO (3rd SERIES)

6 cylinders in line, 2443 cc, 87 hp, twin overhead camshafts. Wheelbase 3250 mm.

ALFA ROMEO
5 SEATER SALOON

Tyres 6.00"x18" on artillery wheels. **Chassis from 913001 to 913169,** **engines from 923001 to 923242 but not in consecutive order.**

The appearance of the 3rd Series, with its 2.5 litre engine developed from the 6C 2300 B, brought the evolution of the 6C project to a close.
The new model incorporated few technical innovations and was designated 3rd Series because it was an evolution of the 6C 2300 B 2nd Series.

The production saloon.

6C 2500 TURISMO (3rd SERIES)

6 cylinders in line, 2443 cc, 87 hp, twin overhead camshafts. Wheelbase 3250 mm.

ALFA ROMEO SALOON
6-7 SEATER,...

This is the 6-7 seater with body by Alfa Romeo destined, as with previous models, for prestige use.
Tyres 6.00"x18" on artillery wheels. **Chassis from 914001 to 914073, engines from 923001 to 923242.**

The production saloon.

6C 2500 SPORT (3rd SERIES)

6 cylinders in line, 2443 cc, 95 hp, twin overhead camshafts. Wheelbase 3000 mm.

Chassis for:

SPORTS TOURER,
CABRIOLET, ROADSTER,...

The Sports version was also presented in Berlin, together with the Turismo and had an engine similar to that of the **6C 2300 B MILLE MIGLIA.** Tyres 5.50"x18" with spoked wheels. **Chassis included between 915001 and 915041, engines between 923801 and 923870 but not in consecutive order.**

Touring coupè.

TIPO 256 (6C 2500 SUPER SPORT)*

6 cylinders in line, 2443 cc, 120 hp, twin overhead camshafts. Wheelbase 2700 mm.

Chassis for:

SPORTS SALOON, SPORTING ROADSTER,...

The chassis and engine numbers of this model, taken from the **3ʳᵈ Series** of the **6C 2500 Sport**, could suggest that the **256** (2500 cc, 6 cylinders) – a designation attributed to Enzo Ferrari – represented a simple elaboration of the basic model for sports purposes. But the profound transformation of the car carried out at Scuderia Ferrari in Modena qualified it as a model in its own right: the car's wheelbase was reduced substantially and its engine power significantly increased, parts of the engine were fusion in *elektron* instead of aluminium and the body was made by Touring. The fact that the car was not reserved for racing drivers alone but that a number with more comfortably fin-

ished bodies were sold to ordinary customers also qualified it for this book. This car also has the merit of having represented the basis for normal production of the **6C 2500 Super Sport** which was officially introduced in 1942 and remained in production until 1952, never-the-

Sports Roadster

less losing part of its mechanical performance.

The chassis still had no central crossbars for more rigidity. Tyres Pirelli Corsa 5.50"x18" with spoked wheels.

Chassis were included between 915001 and 915014 and engines in the numbers of the **6C 2500 Sport**, assigned without progressive order. The chassis used for the **256** in 1939, it was ascertained, were the following: 915006, 915007, 915008, 915009, 915010, 915011, 915014. Others were probably fitted with the same bodies and used for racing.

*As far as Alfa Romeo and Alfa Corse of the period were concerned, the Super Sport designation was rather questionable in that the 6C 2500 Super Sport first saw the light of day in 1942 and assumed its own chassis numbering system; from 1946 the car appeared regularly in the company's price lists.

6C 2500 COLONIALE (3ʳᵈ SERIES)

6 cylinders in line, 2443 cc, 90 hp, twin overhead camshafts. Wheelbase 3100 mm.

ALFA ROMEO TOURER FOR MILITARY USE

A commission from Italy's Ministry of Defence in 1938 gave Alfa Romeo the chance to design a car able to overcome all kinds of obstacles.

Only two prototypes were made in 1939 and they were used for testing.

Tyres 6.50"x19" on artillery wheels. The two prototypes were numbered 916001 and 916002 and the engines 924001 and 924002, but they were officially included in 1941 production.

NO SIGNIFICANT MODIFICATIONS TO THE FOLLOWING MODELS:
6C 2300 B Corto (2ⁿᵈ Series). Chassis from 813399 a 813411; engines included in 823185 e 823650 but not in progressive order.
6C 2300 B Lungo (2ⁿᵈ Series). Chassis from 814317 a 814345; engines included in 823185 e 823650 but not in consecutive order.

COMPETITION CAR NOT FOR PUBLIC SALE
412 - TWO-SEATER SPORTS ROADSTER

1940

NO SIGNIFICANT MODIFICATIONS TO THE FOLLOWING MODELS:

6C 2500 Turismo (3rd Series). Chassis from 913170 to 913232, engines included between 923243 and 923313 but not in consecutive order.

6C 2500 Turismo (3rd Series). Chassis from 914074 to 914081, engines included between 923243 and 923313 in no particular order.

6C 2500 Sport (3rd Series). Chassis included between 915042 and 915110, engines included between 923830 and 923908 but not in consecutive order.

Tipo 256 (6C 2500 Super Sport). Chassis included between 915024 and 915093, engines were included in 6C 2500 Sport numbers, but not in consecutive order. The chassis which were made in 1940, it has been ascertained, were the following: 915024, 915029, 915091, 915092, 915093.

NO PRODUCT EXAMPLE:
6C 2500 Coloniale (3rd Series)

COMPETITION CAR NOT FOR PUBLIC SALE
512 - GRAND PRIX SINGLE-SEATER
158/1940 - GRAND PRIX SINGLE-SEATER

1941

NO SIGNIFICANT MODIFICATIONS TO THE FOLLOWING MODELS:

6C 2500 Turismo (3rd Series). Chassis and engines in 1940 numbers.
6C 2500 Sport (3rd Series). No cars produced.
6C 2500 Coloniale (3rd Series), Chassis from 916003 to 916085, engines from 924003 to 924085.

The 6C 2500 Coloniale shown on the cover of
Alfa Romeo's bi-monthly bulletin.

An advertisement for the 6C 2500 Sport.

1942

6C 2500 TURISMO (3rd SERIES)

6 cylinders in line, 2443 cc, 87 hp, twin overhead camshafts. Wheelbase 3250 mm.

ALFA ROMEO SALOON

During the year a profound modification of the chassis was introduced, starting with number 913236. The chassis was made more rigid with a central cross unit which integrated partially with the cross members.
Chassis from 913233 to 913253 (except 913248, 913249 to 913251), 923323 to 923339 but not in consecutive order*.

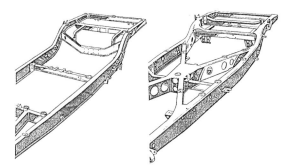

On the right, the chassis updated in 1942.

6C 2500 SPORT (3rd SERIES)

6 cylinders in line, 2443 cc, 95 hp, twin overhead camshafts. Wheelbase 3000 mm.

Chassis for:

SPORTS TOURER, CABRIOLET, ROADSTER,...

From car 915119, the first made in 1942 after production was suspended for a year, the chassis was modified with cross members for greater rigidity.

Chassis from 915119 to 915171; engines from 923920 to 923971 in consecutive order; in addition 915176 and 923972 to 915177 with engine 923973.

6C 2500 SUPER SPORT (3rd SERIE)

6 cylinders in line, 2443 cc, 110 hp, twin overhead camshafts. Wheelbase 2700.

Chassis for:

SPORTS SALOON, CABRIOLET, SPORTS ROADSTER,...

After the experience of 1939, during which the definition Super Sport was not completely official, the 1942 **6C 2500 Super Sport** became an official designation with its own chassis and engine numbers.
The new car benefitted from an updated chassis with central cross members for greater rigidity. The Super Sport was the most sought-after model of the 6C 2500 range and its success enabled Alfa Romeo to produce it, even if with many re-

The Pinin Farina Cabriolet.

visions, until 1951.
Chassis from 915501 to 915522, engines from 923601 to 923622 in consecutive order, in addition with engine 915526, 923626 except the 915517 built in February, 1943.

NO SIGNIFICANT MODIFICATIONS TO THE FOLLOWING MODEL:
6C 2500 Coloniale (3rd Series). Chassis from 916086 to 916152, engines from 924086 to 924152.

1943

NO SIGNIFICANT MODIFICATIONS TO THE FOLLOWING MODELS:

6C 2500 Turismo (3rd Series). Chassis from 913255 to 913269 and from 913271 to 913277 and then 913248, 913249, 913251, 913253, 913279 and 913281, engines from 923242 to 923370 but not in consecutive order.
6C 2500 Sport (3rd Series). Chassis: from 915172 to 915175; from 915178 to 915199 and numbers 915201 and 915202; engines from 923989 to 926002 but not in consecutive order.
6C 2500 Super Sport (3rd Series). Chassis: 915517, 915523, 915524, 915525, 915527, 915528; engines from 923617 to 923628 in consecutive order.

1944

NO SIGNIFICANT MODIFICATIONS TO THE FOLLOWING MODELS:

6C 2500 Turismo (3rd Series). Chassis 913269 with engine 923365, 913278 with engine 923366, 913282 with engine 923367, 913284 with engine 923371.
6C 2500 Sport (3rd Series). Chassis: 915200 with engine 923999 and from 915203 to 915218 with engines from 926004 to 926017, partly in consecutive order.
6C 2500 Super Sport. No cars produced.

The bombing raids of 14 February, 13 August and 20 October reduced Alfa Romeo to a mass of rubble.

THE EVENTS WHICH LED TO POST-WAR RESUMPTION OF OPERATIONS

28 April, 1945:
Ugo Gobbato, the man who saved Alfa Romeo from the requisition of all its raw materials by the Germans, was accused of collaboration. Acquitted twice by the tribunal of the Committee of National Liberation, he was assassinated three days after the liberation of Milan. His killers were two armed individuals who climbed out of a Lancia Augusta, one with a military rifle and another with a shot gun, who escaped after the shooting.

End of May, 1945:
The Committee of National Liberation nominated Ing. Pasquale Gallo commissioner extraordinary of Alfa Romeo.

June – July, 1945
In the factories, partially re-activated production of the **6C 2500 Sport** resumed, but with only two chassis assembled by the end of the year.

With the establishment of the Republic, the Alfa Romeo badge (above left) was completely re-designed and produced in metal only. Obviously, parts of the design linked to the House of Savoy were eliminated and substituted with two wavy lines. In 1950, with the arrival of the 1900, the Alfa badge went back to its pre-war appearance (top right) without, of course, the Savoy insignia and was once again made in brass and enamel.

1945

NO SIGNIFICANT MODIFICATIONS TO THE FOLLOWING MODELS:
6C 2500 Sport (3ʳᵈ Series). Chassis 915219 with engine 929020 and 915220 with engine 926019.
6C 2500 Super Sport. No cars produced.

1946

6C 2500 SPORT LUNGO

(TYPE 1947, ENGINE TYPE 6C 2500 TURISMO)

6 cylinders in line, 2443 cc, 87 hp, twin overhead camshafts. Wheelbase 3250 mm.

ALFA ROMEO SALOON
AND
CHASSIS FOR
CABRIOLET AND COUPE'

In March bodies for the Sport Lungo, new name for the Turismo which ceased production in 1944, were built in-house, while those for the Sport were commissioned outside: Touring, Pinin Farina, Stabilimenti Farina, Bertone, Castagna, Boneschi (photo) etc.
Chassis and engines: 913254 with engine 923379 (perhaps a prototype); from 913285 to 913363 engines included from 923378 to 923460.

6C 2500 SUPER SPORT (3rd SERIES)

(TYPE 1947, ENGINE TYPE 6C 2500 SUPER SPORT)

6 cylinders in line, 2443 cc, 110 hp, twin overhead camshafts. Wheelbase 2700 mm.

Chassis for:

SPORTS SALOON,
CABRIOLET,

COUPE', ROADSTER

No Super Sport chassis were produced in 1944 and 1945: Alfa

Romeo's top-of-the-range model reappeared in July, its characteristics almost identical to the last cars to be produced in 1943.
Chassis from 915529to 915542.

A Pinin Farina Cabriolet built for the crown prince of Sweden.

The Pinin Farina Cabriolet.

_ 6C 2500 SPORT FRECCIA D'ORO _

(TYPE 1947, ENGINE TYPE 6C 2500 SPORT)

6 cylinders in line, 2443 cc, 90 hp, twin overhead camshafts. Wheelbase 3000 mm.

ALFA ROMEO 2 DOOR SALOON

This was the first post-war project, even though it is a close relation of the 6C 2500. The chassis of the previous **6C 2500 Sport** (wheelbase 3000 mm) was modified by placing the gear lever on the steering column in line with the fashion of the day, the steel body-frame was welded to the chassis. Engine power was reduced by 5 hp, compared to the previous series.
Chassis and engines: 915239 with engine 926077 (called the experi- mental saloon, almost certainly the model's prototype, the chassis of which was finished on 26.9.46. and sold as a used car in 1952).

B.000816

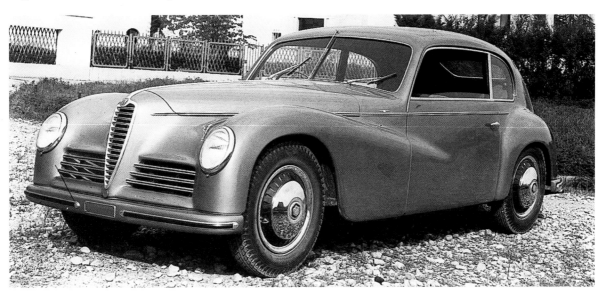

NO SIGNIFICANT MODIFICATIONS TO THE FOLLOWING MODELS, WITH THE EXCEP-
TION OF VARIATIONS TO THE BODYWORK :

6C 2500 Sport (3rd Series). Chassis and engines: from 915221 to 915284 (except 915270 with engine 926264, 926082, 915274 with engine 926112, 915279, 926093, 915280, 926056 destined for Touring and Pinin Farina and built in 1947), engines included between 926021 and 926112.

COMPETITION CAR NOT FOR PUBLIC SALE
158/47 - GRAND PRIX SINGLE SEATER.

NO SIGNIFICANT MODIFICATIONS TO THE FOLLOWING MODELS, WITH THE EXCEPTION OF VARIATIONS IN THE BODYWORK

6C 2500 Sport Freccia D'Oro (1947 Type)
In September, the Gazzella new car project started in 1945 was abandoned. It would have seen the introduction of a new load-bearing body shell (photo below right). Production began of the Freccia D'Oro (photo right), which can be considered the first real post-war Alfa, even though it retained close links with the pre-war 6C 2500.
Chassis included between 915254 e 916004.
Chassis included between 926036 and 927247, but not in consecutive order.
6C 2500 Sport (1947 type). Chassis included between 915285 and 916040.

NO SIGNIFICANT MODIFICATIONS TO THE MECHANICS OF THE FOLLOWING MODELS; VARIATIONS TO THE BODYWORK:
6C 2500 Sport Lungo (type 1947). Chassis included between 913364 and 913367.
6C 2500 Super Sport (type 1947). Chassis from 915543 to 915613. (photo below)

Touring Super Sport Coupè

_ 6C 2500 SPORT FRECCIA D'ORO _
(TYPE 1947, ENGINE TYPE 6C 2500 SPORT)
6 cylinders in line, 2443 cc, 90 hp, twin overhead camshafts. Wheelbase 3000 mm.

**ALFA ROMEO
2 DOOR SALOON**

The front was updated to include new lateral louvers, central shield with vertical slats and new headlights.
Chassis included between 915466 and 916306. Engines included between 926036 and 927247.

The Freccia D'Oro production line.

NO SIGNIFICANT MODIFICATIONS TO THE FOLLOWING MODELS, WITH THE EXCEPTION OF VARIATIONS TO THE BODYWORK:
6C 2500 Sport (1947 type). Chassis included between 916059 and 916422.
6C 2500 Sport Lungo (1947 type). Chassis: from 913368 to 913392, engines included between 923461 and 926733 (except 913370 with engine 923472, produced in 1944).
6C 2500 Super Sport (1947 type). Chassis: from 915614 to 915717 (except 915701 which was demolished), engines included between 923714 and 923798 and between 928002 and 928022.

COMPETITION CAR NOT FOR PUBLIC SALE
6C 2500 COMPETIZIONE - SPORTING SALOON FOR ROAD AND TRACK RACES

6C 2500 TURISMO MOTORE AVANZATO
(TYPE 1949, ENGINE TYPE 6C 2500 TURISMO)

6 cylinders in line, 2443 cc, 87 hp, twin overhead camshafts. Wheelbase 3250 mm.

Chassis for:

SALOON

Moving the engine and gearbox forward with appropriate chassis modifications allowed the fitment of large, six-seater bodies (in the photo a body by Stabilimenti Farina). **Chassis included between 913395 and 913247.** Engines included between 926824 and 926997.

6C 2500 SPORT MOTORE AVANZATO
(TYPE 1950, ENGINE TYPE 6C 2500 SPORT)

6 cylinders in line, 2443 cc, 90 hp, twin overhead camshafts. Wheelbase 3000 mm.

Chassis for:

SALOON

As had already happened with the 6C 2500 Turismo, the engine-gearbox group of this model was also moved forward to allow larger bodies to be fitted. **Chassis included between 917001 and 917053.** Engines included between 926778 and 927034 (in the photo a Pinin Farina-bodied car).

6C 2500 SPORT FRECCIA D'ORO
(TYPE 1950, ENGINE TYPE 6C 2500 SPORT)

6 cylinders in line, 2443 cc, 90 hp, twin overhead camshafts. Wheelbase 3000 mm.

ALFA ROMEO SALOON

The bumper bars were given new guards, the side and rear windows were enlarged. Fog lights were also introduced. **Chassis included between 916265 and 916554.**

NO SIGNIFICANT MODIFICATIONS TO THE FOLLOWING MODELS, EXCEPT FOR VARIATIONS TO THE BODYWORK:

6C 2500 Sport (type 1947). Chassis included between 916427 and 916446.
6C 2500 Sport Lungo (type 1947). Chassis 913393 and 913394.
6C 2500 Super Sport (type 1947). Chassis from 915718 to 915890.

6C 2500 SPORT MOTORE SUPER SPORT (GRAN TURISMO)

(TYPE 1948, ENGINE TYPE 6C 2500 SUPER SPORT)

6 cylinders in line, 2443 cc, 110 hp, twin overhead camshafts. Wheelbase 3000 mm.

ALFA ROMEO SALOON AND CHASSIS FOR COUPE', CABRIOLET

The production model.

This was a lot of almost 150 **6C 2500 Sport**-type cars fitted with Super Sport engines. The model was called **6C 2500 Gran Turismo**. **Chassis from 918001 to 918150.**

1900

(TYPE 1483, ENGINE TYPE AR1306)

4 cylinders in line, 1884 cc, 80 hp, twin overhead camshafts. Wheelbase 2630 mm

ALFA ROMEO SALOON, COUPE',...

By 1950, the 6C 2500 had become outmoded and Alfa Romeo believed it was time to develop a more modern, more revolutionary car in step with the new technology of the day including the car body integrated into the chassis, a forerunner of the full load-bearing body shell. The engine was also simplified; the company opted for a four cylinder of simpler concept and lower fiscal cost. But mechanical refinement was not penalised because the twin overhead camshaft and that type of technology, tested in motor sport and by this time part of the Alfa Romeo tradition, were retained. So performance was high. The **1900** was a true technical turning point, which established the company's future tradition. It was the first car completely designed and developed under Orazio Satta. Carburettor: Solex 33 PBIC, Solex 40 PAI, Weber 40 DCF5, which gave the car respectively 80, 85 and 90 hp. The Weber 40 DCL5 and 40 DCZ5 were also adopted. **Chassis included between AR1900*00001 and *00006.**

NO SIGNIFICANT MODIFICATION TO THE FOLLOWING MODELS, WITH THE EXCEPTION OF BODYWORK VARIATIONS:
6C 2500 Sport (type 1947). Chassis 916691 (one car built).
6C 2500 Sport Freccia D'Oro (type 1950). Chassis included between 916499 and 916690.
6C 2500 Turismo Motore Avanzato (type 1949). Chassis from 913428 to 913445.
6C 2500 Sport Motore Avanzato (type 1950). Chassis included between 917026 and 917149.
6C 2500 Super Sport (1947 type). Chassis from 915891 to 915907.

COMPETITION CAR NOT FOR PUBLIC SALE
6C 3000 C50 - SPORTS SALOON FOR ROAD AND TRACK RACING

1900 C SPRINT
(TYPE 1484, ENGINE TYPE AR1308)

4 cylinders in line, 1884 cc, 100 hp, twin overhead camshafts. Wheelbase 2500 mm.

Chassis for:

COUPE', CABRIOLET,...

Coupè Touring.

In 1951, a chassis was developed for bodies 13 cm shorter than that of the **1900** saloon (the C stands for corto or short, but the body-builders had different ideas). The engine became notably more powerful and the twin choke Weber 40 DCA3 carburettor was adopted The 40DCL3 and 40DCZ3 were also planned. The gearbox was four speed with the lever on the steering column, although Nardi of Turin developed an interesting modification with an floor-mounted gear lever.

According to an Alfa Romeo work order, the coupè bodies were produced, in particular, by Touring while the cabriolet were built almost exclusively by Pinin Farina (photo right) as well as a number of elegant coupès.

The first examples of the Touring coupè incorporated a door which reached down to the base of the body (photo above) while the small bumper bars were soon replaced by larger units with guards.

Seats were either in real or imitation leather and cloth.

AR1900C*00053,

Pinin Farina Cabriolét.

NO SIGNIFICANT MODIFICATIONS TO THE FOLLOWING MODELS:
1900 (type 1483). Chassis included between AR1900*00037 and *11237.
6C 2500 Sport Freccia D'Oro (type 1950). Chassis 916692 (only one car produced).
6C 2500 Sport con Motore Super Sport (type 1948). Chassis from 918001 to 918051.
6C 2500 con Motore Avanzato (type 1950). Chassis 917150 and 917151.
6C 2500 Super Sport (type 1947). Chassis from 915908 to 915925.

COMPETITION CARS NOT FOR PUBLIC SALE
159 - GRAND PRIX SINGLE-SEATER - **1900 C GARA** - SPORTS SALOON FOR ROAD AND TRACK RACING.

1900 M (AR 51)
(TYPE 1412, ENGINE TYPE AR1307)
4 cylinders in line, 1884 cc, 65 hp, twin overhead camshafts. Wheelbase 2200 mm.

ALFA ROMEO TOURER

In this case, AR does not stand for Alfa Romeo but Autovettura da Ricognizione or recognisance vehicle; it is based on a formula devised by Italy's Ministry of Defence and given to Alfa Romeo to build a vehicle able to overcome all obstacles. Also irreverently called the "Alfa Matta" (Mad Alfa), it was the forebear of the modern off-roader. The company delivered 2000 ARs to the Ministry and 50 were produced for civil use. The AR remained in production until 1954, when it became known as the AR 52. Chassis included between **AR51*00001 and *00761.**

1900 L
(TYPE 1483, ENGINE TYPE AR1306)
4 cylinders in line, 1884 cc, 80 hp, twin overhead camshafts. Wheelbase 2630 mm.

Chassis for:

COUPE', CABRIOLET,…

A special car chassis was developed for the bodybuilders in 1952. Its wheelbase and track were for a saloon but the platform was suitable for larger dimensions, both in length and width. This chassis was used by Stabilimenti Farina, Bertone, Ghia, Pinin Farina and Boneschi. Some became the 1900 T.I. Some were made to 1900 T.I. specifications. **Chassis from AR1900*00071 to *00079, from AR1900*10070 to *10079, from AR1900*20070 to *20079, from AR1900*30070 to *30079, from AR1900*40070 to *40079, from AR1900*50070 to *50071, from AR1900*01052 to *01062, from AR1900*01065 to *01069. 1900 L T.I. Chassis AR1900*01063, *01064, from AR1900*01066 to *01068, *01070, *01071.**

1900 C SPRINT
(TYPE 1484, ENGINE TYPE AR1308)
4 cylinders in line, 1884 cc, 100 hp, twin overhead camshafts. Wheelbase 2500 mm.

Chassis for:

COUPE', CABRIOLET,…

A conventional under door was introduced on the Touring coupè and the door was reduced in the lower part. Other small modifications to the interior. The Pinin Farina Cabriolet's front wings were also slightly modified and became rounder, but the most evident revision was to the door handles. No changes were made to either car's mechanics. **Chassis included between AR1900C*00051 and *00059, between AR1900C*01018 and *01132, between AR1900C*01201 and *01270, between AR1900C*10051 and *10057.**

NO SIGNIFICANT MODIFICATION TO THE FOLLOWING MODELS, WITH THE EXCEPTION OF BODYWORK VARIATIONS TO THE 6C 2500:
1900 (type 1483). Chassis included between AR1900*12330 and *91539 and from AR1900*01600 to *04320.
6C 2500 Sport Motore Super Sport (type 1948). Chassis included between 918083 and 918146.

COMPETITION CARS NOT FOR PUBLIC SALE
1900 C52 - SPORTS SALOON AND ROADSTER FOR ROAD AND TRACK RACING - **6C 3000 CM** - SPORTS SALOON AND ROADSTER FOR ROAD AND TRACK RACING - TIPO **160** - GRAND PRIX SINGLE-SEATER

1900 T.I.
(TYPE 1483, ENGINE TYPE AR1306)
4 cylinders in line, 1884 cc, 100 hp, twin overhead camshafts. Wheelbase 2630 mm.

ALFA ROMEO SALOON,…

A total of 572 **1900**s were modified to compete in the International Touring Car category (T.I.).
The model is recognisable by its two Solex 40 PII carburettors (Weber 40 DCO3 horizontal carburettors were also used), the steel tube racing exhausts and the large diameter drum brakes which were also adopted for the Super Sprint.
The **1900 T.I.** was not given its own numbering system because the body shell came from normal **1900** production and was converted to T.I. specifications.

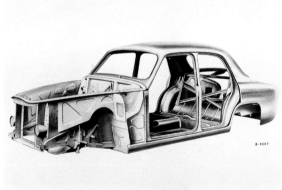

Body shell of the 1900.

NO SIGNIFICANT MODIFICATIONS TO THE FOLLOWING MODELS, WITH THE EXCEPTION OF BODY VARIATIONS TO THE 6C 2500:

1900 (type 1483). Chassis included between AR1900*04321 and *07475.

1900 C Sprint (type 1484). Chassis included between AR1900C*00054 and *01653.

1900 L (type 1483). Chassis AR1900*00076, *00079, *10075, *20077, from AR1900C*30070 to *30072, *30075, *30078, from AR1900C*40072 to *40079, from AR1900C*40075 a *40079.

1900 M (AR51) (type 1412). Chassis from AR51*00762 to *01506.

6C 2500 Sport Motore Super Sport (type 1948). Chassis 918109, 918110, 918147 (the last 6C 2500 was produced on 26-10-53)

1954

1900 SUPER
(TYPE 1483, ENGINE TYPE AR1306)

4 cylinders in line, 1975 cc, 90 hp, twin overhead camshafts. Wheelbase 2630 mm.

ALFA ROMEO SALOON,
COUPE',…

To create a more powerful and reliable engine, the bore was increased by 2 mm while the stroke remained the same. A Solex 40 PAI carburettor was fitted. After the first body, which hardly differentiated this model from the others – new rear optical group and wheels with oval 'windows' to improve brake cooling, a feature which had already appeared on the **1900** saloon – two new elements were introduced which would stay with the car until it went out of production: a strip along the side panels and the **1900 Super** script.
From production start-up, the dashboard was fitted with round instruments and the seats were covered with cloth and imitation leather.
Engine numbers began at AR1306*13151.
Chassis included between AR1900*08001 and *09999, and from AR1900*12000 to *12944.

1900 T.I. SUPER
(TYPE 1483, ENGINE TYPE AR1306)

4 cylinders in line, 1975 cc, 115 hp, twin overhead camshafts. Wheelbase 2630 mm.

ALFA ROMEO SALOON,
COUPE',…

This car is nothing a **1900 T.I.**, but fitted with a new 1975 cc Super series engine which would also be used for the **1900 C Super Sprint**. Carburettors: twin Solex 40 PII identical to those of the 1900 T.I. Competition exhausts and large diameter drum brakes.
The **1900 T.I. Super** had no numbering system of its own because the body shells were taken from normal **1900 Super** production and modified to T.I. specifications. Photo: a Pinin Farina coupè.

1900 M (AR52)
(TYPE 1412, ENGINE TYPE AR1307)

4 cylinders in line, 1884 cc, 65 hp, twin overhead camshafts. Wheelbase 2200 mm.

ALFA ROMEO TOURER

The model name was changed to AR52 without significant technical modifications.
Chassis from AR52*00001 to *00154.

1900 C SUPER SPRINT
(TYPE 1484, ENGINE TYPE AR1308)
4 cylinders in line, 1975 cc, 115 hp, twin overhead camshafts. Wheelbase 2500 mm.

Chassis for:

COUPE', CABRIOLET,...

This car was an evolution of the **1900 C Sprint** for which Carrozzeria Touring built the bodies (coupè version) and was fitted with the Super engine approaching two litres. The glass area was increased, in particular the rear window and the side lights (in plexiglass). The door handles were of different design and the original equipment fog lamps were located at the sides of the central shield. The Brunsig bumpers had already been fitted to many of the **1900 C Sprint** cars.
Carburettors: 2 Solex 40 PII identical to those of the **1900 T.I.** and T.I. Super, but fitted with a different steel blade filter. Five speed gearbox with the lever on the steering column. Seats in imitation leather and cloth.
Chassis included between AR1900C*01654 and *01964.

Touring coupè.

GIULIETTA SPRINT
(TYPE 750 B, ENGINE TYPE AR1315)
4 cylinders in line, 1290 cc, 65 hp, twin overhead camshafts. Wheelbase 2380 mm.

BERTONE COUPE'

Without doubt one of the most successful Alfa Romeos, the **Giulietta Sprint** signalled the commitment of the company in the medium power segment.
With this extremely successful car, the Alfa Romeo sporting tradition was given a surprising re-launch and 11 years of the car's production bear testimony to that fact.
The mechanics came from competition in that their design and development were carried out by the same technicians who tested the company's racing cars. Twin overhead camshafts, all-light alloy engine, gearbox and differential made the car a technical sensation, the watershed of a whole dynasty of mechanical components which continued through into the Nineties.
Seats in vertically striped cloth, roof panel covering in cloth and woollen carpet for the floor. Carburettor: Solex C 32 PAIAT.
Chassis included between AR1493*00001 and *00012.

The pre-production version. Note the petrol tank cap.

The final version.

NO SIGNIFICANT MODIFICATIONS TO THE FOLLOWING MODELS:
1900 (type 1483). Chassis included between AR1900*07476 and *08000.
1900 C Sprint (type 1484). Chassis included between AR1900C*01121 and 01556.
1900 L (type 1483). Chassis from AR1900*01072 to *01084; from AR1900*01086 to 01088.
1900 L T.I. (type 1483). Chassis from AR1900*01085 to *01089.
1900 M (AR 51) (type 1412). Chassis from AR51*01507 to *01913; from AR51*50001 to *50005.

COMPETITION CARS NOT FOR PUBLIC SALE
6C 3000 PR - TWO-SEATER SPORTS CAR FOR ROAD AND TRACK RACING - **1900 SPORT** - TWO-SEATER SPORTS
- **2000 SPORTIVA** - SPORTS SALOON

1900 SUPER
(TYPE 1483, ENGINE TYPE AR1306)
4 cylinders in line, 1975 cc, 90 hp, twin overhead camshafts. Wheelbase 2630 mm.

ALFA ROMEO SALOON,
COUPE',...

From the spring of 1955, the car's power distribution was modified by the adoption of two silent chains in the place of the previous system of toothed wheel and chain. The rotation direction of the cams was reversed and the firing order was modified from 1-3-4-2 to 1-2-4-3. **Chassis included between AR1900*12945 and *15120.**

GIULIETTA
(TYPE 750 C, ENGINE TYPE AR1315)
4 cylinders in line, 1290 cc, 50 hp, twin overhead camshafts. Wheelbase 2380 mm.

ALFA ROMEO SALOON

After a spasmodic delay, it was decided this car would be launched before the Sprint; it was unveiled at the Turin Motor Show in April, 1955, and became an instant success. It was built on the coupe's platform, had an engine of reduced power and a saloon body with four comfortable seats. **Chassis included between AR1488*00002 and *01464.** The engine numbering system began at AR1315*50001.

GIULIETTA SPIDER
(TYPE 750 D, ENGINE TYPE AR1315)
4 cylinders in line, 1290 cc, 65 hp, twin overhead camshafts. Wheelbase 2200 mm.

PININ FARINA ROADSTER

The production of the Giulietta Spider was commissioned by American importer Max Hoffman. Carrozzeria Pinin Farina won the contract and proposed to Alfa a body which was so beautiful and equilibrated that it created a whole new fashion.

The car was first displayed at the Frankfurt Motor Show in the autumn of 1955 but did not become immediately available in Italy as the American requirements were met first. The cars made that year were prototypes and pre-series examples which included bodies by Bertone (chassis AR1495*00002 and 00004, the latter officially dated 1956), while AR1495*00007, the almost definitive version, was exhibited at shows. **Chassis AR1495*00002, *00003, *00007, *00011.**
Engine numbers began at AR1315*40001.

GIULIETTA SPRINT
(TYPE 750 B, ENGINE TYPE AR1315)
4 cylinders in line, 1290 cc, 65 hp, twin overhead camshafts. Wheelbase 2380 mm.

BERTONE COUPE'

Many mechanical modifications were adopted during the year.
From engine number AR1315*00997, the Solex 35 APAIG carburettor replaced the Solex C 32 PAIAT.
From engine AR1315*01051, the filter was substituted by another of cylindrical shape.
From car AR1493*00551, the rear cluster included a reversing light.
Chassis included between AR1493*00013 and *01421.

NO SIGNIFICANT MODIFICATIONS TO THE FOLLOWING MODELS:

1900 L (type 1483). Chassis, AR1900*01092, *01093
1900 Super (type 1483). Chassis included between AR1900*12945 and *15120.
1900 T.I. Super (type 1483). Chassis included between AR1900*13001 and *15610.
1900C Super Sprint. (1ˢᵗ example) (**type 1484**). Chassis included between AR1900C*01965 and *02195.

COMPETITION CAR NOT FOR PUBLIC SALE
750 COMPETIZIONE - SPORTS TWO-SEATER

GIULIETTA SPRINT VELOCE
(TYPE 750 E, ENGINE TYPE AR1315)
4 cylinders in line, 1290 cc, 90 hp, twin overhead camshafts. Wheelbase 2380 mm.

BERTONE COUPE'

To compete in the 1956 Mille Miglia, Alfa Romeo developed a car which could beat the Porsches. The project was an enormous success, so much so that the lightweight **Giulietta**, initially built to qualify the car for homologation, ended up not being produced until mid-1958.
Extremely high performance: the engine with single feed by two Weber 40 DCO3 carburettors (more or less a carburettor for each cylinder), racing exhausts and dynamic air intake feed immediately increased the car's power by 30%. The bonnet, boot lid and doors were made of light alloy, the latter with sliding plexiglass windows as with the rest of the car except for the windscreen, reducing weight by 20%.
The body shell came from the **Giulietta Sprint**, so the Veloce did not have its own chassis numbering system but did have a stamped E between AR1493 and the consecutive number, which indicated the specific type.
Engine numbers, assigned in no particular order, begin at AR1315*30001 and were the same as the **Giulietta Spider Veloce**. The crankcases of these particular engines like those initially used for the Sprint, were reinforced between the second and third cylinders, which connect the two walls.
Chassis included between AR1493E*01380 and *03599.

GIULIETTA SPIDER VELOCE
(TYPE 750 F, ENGINE TYPE AR1315)
4 cylinders in line, 1290 cc, 90 hp, twin overhead camshafts. Wheelbase 2200 mm.

PININ FARINA ROADSTER

As with the Sprint, the Spider was modified but, with the exception of replacing the large bumper guards with smaller units, the car's aesthetics remained unchanged.
Apart from competition in the U.S.A., this car was not used for racing: that was the job of the Sprint Veloce and is why the car was not a lightweight: it was 5 kilos heavier than the Spider. Compared to the standard model, the only modification was to the scale of the instruments (rev counter maximum 8000 rpm, speedometer 220 km/h).
The engine (AR 1315) constituted a single lot together with those fitted to the Sprint Veloce.

Chassis included in the Giulietta Spider numbering system.

1900 C SUPER SPRINT

(TYPE 1484, ENGINE TYPE AR1308)

4 cylinders in line, 1975 cc, 115 hp, twin overhead camshafts. Wheelbase 2500 mm.

chassis for:

COUPE', CABRIOLET

Touring coupè

The second version of the **1900 C Super Sprint** was, perhaps, the most elegant and successful. It was also the last example of the 1900 C and the construction of its body was, once again, entrusted to Carrozzeria Touring.

The Milan atelier pulled off a real miracle, greatly reducing height and producing a modern and desirable car.

The gear lever for the five speed box could also be mounted on the floor. Carburettors: 2 Solex 40 PII, the same as the previous version but fitted with an *elektron* filter instead of a steel blade.

Seats in cloth and leather, as with the doors decorated with an oblique cut design: the lower section had a document pocket. Wool carpeting. Also of interest were the small number of very aggressive coupès built by Carrozzeria Zagato, as attractive as the cabriolet (perhaps only one example) built both by Touring and Zagato.

The engines, similar in appearance and of the same performance level, have a specific numerical sequence beginning with AR1308*10002.

For identification purposes, the new car's chassis did not follow the previous numbering system.

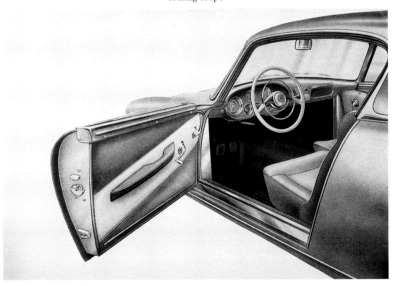

Chassis included between AR1900C*10001 and *10344.

NO SIGNIFICANT MODIFICATION TO THE FOLLOWING MODELS:

Giulietta (type 750 C). Chassis included between AR1488*01219 and *07780.
Giulietta Sprint (type750 B). Chassis included between AR1493*01352 and *03583.
Giulietta Spider (type 750 D). Chassis AR1495*00004 (2ⁿᵈ Bertone prototype) and included between AR1495*00005 and *01090.
1900 L (type 1483). Chassis AR1900*01094, *01095.
1900 T.I. Super (type 1483). Chassis: AR1900*14983, *14996; from AR1900*15501 to *15506, *15528.
1900 Super (type 1483). Chassis included between AR1900*15121 and *17550.
1900 C Super Sprint (1ˢᵗ version) **(type 1484).** Chassis AR1900C*02130, *02143, *02145, *02189.

GIULIETTA PROMISCUA
(TYPE 750 C, ENGINE TYPE AR1315)

4 cylinders in line, 1290 cc, 50 hp, twin overhead camshafts. Wheelbase 2380 mm.

COLLI STATION WAGON

Carrozzeria Colli of Milan was commissioned to produce the Promiscua, an interesting car-type *station wagon* experiment. It appears that only one example was produced in 1957.
Chassis included in the saloon numbering system.

GIULIETTA
(TYPE 750 C, ENGINE TYPE AR1315)

4 cylinders in line, 1290 cc, 50 hp, twin overhead camshafts. Wheelbase 2380.

ALFA ROMEO SALOON

In June and from chassis number AR1488*11501, modifications were made to the starter motor with electro-magnetic engagement in the area of the mechanical drive. **Chassis included between AR1488*07649 and *16806.**

GIULIETTA SPIDER
(TYPE 750 D, ENGINE TYPE AR1315)

4 cylinders in line, 1290 cc, 65 hp, twin overhead camshafts. Wheelbase 2200 mm.

GIULIETTA SPIDER VELOCE
(TYPE 750 F, ENGINE TYPE AR1315)

4 cylinders in line, 1290 cc, 90 hp, twin overhead camshafts. Wheelbase 2200 mm.

PININ FARINA ROADSTER

From car number AR1495*02208, both the Spider and Spider Veloce were fitted with doors with fixed butterfly window. However, until car AR1495*07213 (1959) production went ahead by fitting doors without such windows.

The seats were smooth, without stitching and in imitation leather. Wool carpeting and mats in grooved rubber with the Alfa Romeo logo.
No mechanical modifications for either model.
Chassis included between AR1495*01084 and *03244.

GIULIETTA t.i.
(TYPE 753, ENGINE TYPE AR1315)
4 cylinders in line, 1290 cc, 65 hp, twin overhead camshafts. Wheelbase 2380 mm.

ALFA ROMEO SALOON

Presented at the Monza race track on 2 September, 1957, the car's performance impressed, given that its power was that of a Sprint but that the Giulietta t.i. was heavier.
Compared to the saloon, the speedometer registered a maximum of 160 km/h and a rev counter was fitted. The aesthetic appearance and bodywork remained unmodified until the Frankfurt Motor Show in September, 1959, while mechanical improvements were the same as those made to the saloon. The internal covering was the typical black and white *pied de poule*.
Engine numbers started at AR1315*80001.
Chassis included between AR1468*00001 and *01503.

GIULIETTA SPRINT
(TYPE 750 B, ENGINE TYPE AR1315)
4 cylinders in line, 1290 cc, 65 hp, twin overhead camshafts. Wheelbase 2380 mm.

BERTONE COUPE'

From car AR1493*05801, asymmetric headlights were introduced with larger capping.
The seating material was again decorated with vertical stripes.
Chassis included between AR1493*01990 and *06090.

NO SIGNIFICANT MODIFICATIONS TO THE FOLLOWING MODELS:
Giulietta Sprint Veloce (type 750 E). Chassis included between AR1493*03448 and *05806.
1900 Super (type AR1483). Chassis included between AR1900*17551 and *19089.
1900 T.I. Super (type 1483). Chassis from AR1900*17644 to *17653; from AR1900* 17741 to *17750; from AR1900*17921 to *17935; from AR1900*18051 to *18065; from AR1900*18251 to *18265; from AR1900*18401 to 18415; from AR1900*18571 to *18590.
1900 C Super Sprint (2nd version) **(type AR1484).** Chassis included between AR1900C*10271 and *10596.

GIULIETTA
(TYPE 750 C, ENGINE TYPE AR1315)

4 cylinders in line, 1290 cc, 53 hp, twin overhead camshafts. Wheelbase 2380 mm.

ALFA ROMEO SALOON

From January and chassis number AR1488*17701, power was increased from 50 to 53 hp. Larger asymmetric headlights were installed with new capping. No other aesthetic modifications.
At the end of September and starting from chassis number AR1488*20801, faster new gears were adopted with the box able to be dismantled from the bell and Porsche-type synchronisers. At the same time, the front suspension was reinforced with small tanks of lubrication grease.
From November and chassis number AR1488*21722, a new hourglass screw steering box was fitted.

Chassis included between AR1488*16460 and *22511.

GIULIETTA t.i.
(TYPE 753, ENGINE TYPE AR1315)

4 cylinders in line, 1290 cc, 65 hp, twin overhead camshafts. Wheelbase 2380 mm.

ALFA ROMEO SALOON

The t.i.'s gearbox and suspension were modified at the same time as the saloon and from chassis number AR1468*08501 (September, 1958). The new hourglass screw steering box was introduced with chassis AR1468*09909. No aesthetic modifications, except the adoption of asymmetric headlights but of the same earlier size.
Chassis included between AR1468*00960 and *11257.

GIULIETTA SPRINT SPECIALE
(TYPE 101.20, ENGINE TYPE AR00120)

4 cylinders in line, 1290 cc, 100 hp, twin overhead camshafts. Wheelbase 2250 mm.

BERTONE COUPE'

The **Giulietta Sprint Speciale** was introduced on 30 October, 1957, but factory records show no trace of the first example. Three prototypes were noted in 1958. The body was in aluminium and the irrepressible design by Franco Scaglione was much more aggressive than the shape of the definitive version, made in sheet steel.
The engine numbering system started at AR00120*00001. Up until AR00120*00200 they maintained the characteristics of the type AR1315 (identified by number 30001 onwards) fitted to the Sprint Veloce type 750 E and Spider Veloce type 750 F, with reduced diameter main journal and head slightly narrower, with valves with stems of 8 mm in diameter. The carburettors were two Weber 40 DCO3.
Chassis AR10120*00002, *00006, *00012.

GIULIETTA SPRINT VELOCE
(TYPE 750 E, ENGINE TYPE AR1315)
4 cylinders in line, 1290 cc, 90 hp, twin overhead camshafts. Wheelbase 2380 mm.

BERTONE COUPE'

A small series of the **Giulietta Sprint Veloce** (May-June, 1958) officially designated Confortevole (Comfortable) at a time when it seems the Sprint Speciale with its light alloy body was to take its place in competition, adopted the doors and glass of the Sprint for easier touring use. The car was also fitted with the larger headlights of the 1957 Sprint.

Some of the early examples still had aluminium frames to the lateral windows.

Mechanics and performance remained unchanged.

The car was given a new steering box and reinforced front suspension. Production records do not show which examples were fitted with these modifications.

From chassis number AR1495*07442, a new gearbox was introduced with Porsche-type synchronisers.

GIULIETTA SPRINT
(TYPE 750 B, ENGINE TYPE AR1315)
4 cylinders in line, 1290 cc, 80 hp, twin overhead camshafts. Wheelbase 2380 mm.

BERTONE COUPE'

From car number AR1493*06601 the exhaust manifold was modified so that it no longer had four in one but four in two outlets and the power was increased noticeably. From AR1493*07301 the Porsche-type synchroniser was fitted, the box could be dismantled from the bell and the lever was located on the floor. From car AR1493*07209, the steering box was replaced by the hourglass screw and roller system, the front suspension became more robust and was given the new, more effective greasing system, which was introduced on the other **Giulietta** models at the same time.

Many aesthetic modifications: the front grills became definitive, the rear lights were enlarged and remained that way until the end of production, while number plate illumination remained unchanged. The seats were in vertically lined material and finished in leather.

Chassis included between AR1493*05637 and *08000.

The lateral flashers were moved further back on the definitive version.

GIULIETTA SPIDER

(TYPE 750 D, ENGINE TYPE AR1315)

4 cylinders in line, 1290 cc, 80 hp, twin overhead camshafts. Wheelbase 2200 mm.

PININ FARINA ROADSTER

A new split exhaust manifold system (see drawing) was adopted from vehicle number AR1495*04256 onwards and the car was given the same power increase as the Sprint. From car AR1495*04811, the gearbox was modified, the suspension made more robust and fitted with grease tanks.
No aesthetic modifications. Doors

with and without butterfly windows continued to be fitted
Chassis included between AR1495*03230 and *05639.

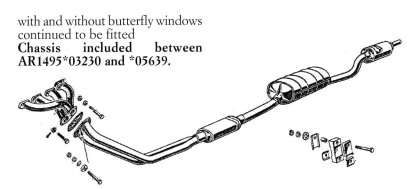

GIULIETTA SPIDER VELOCE

(TYPE 750 F, ENGINE TYPE AR1315)

4 cylinders in line, 1290 cc, 90 hp, twin overhead camshafts. Wheelbase 2200 mm.

PININ FARINA ROADSTER

With the exception of power which remained unchanged, the Spider Veloce received all the modifications to the gearbox and suspension made to the other models.

Chassis included in the Giulietta Spider numbering system.

2000

(TYPE 102.00, ENGINE TYPE AR00200)

4 cylinders in line, 1975 cc, 105 hp, twin overhead camshafts. Wheelbase 2720 mm.

ALFA ROMEO SALOON

The intention of extending the life of the 1900 was put into practice with this new car, which maintained the cubic capacity of the 1900 Super but adopted a new cylinder head with valve drive with interposition of oil bath bowls, the same solution as that for the Giulietta. The body, of considerable dimensions, was homologated for six seats. The car did not sell well and was mainly used for prestige purposes.
Chassis included between AR10200*00004 and *00386.

2000 SPIDER

(TYPE 102.04, ENGINE TYPE AR00204)

4 cylinders in line, 1975 cc, 115 hp, twin overhead camshafts. Wheelbase 2500 mm.

TOURING ROADSTER

Carrozzeria Touring produced the **2000** Spider. The platform of the **1900 C Super Sprint** was suitably updated and used, resulting in a car which was elegant but in the somewhat dubious taste of American style, which characterised Italian car production of the period. It was not modified until mid-1962, although a 2+2 was introduced in July, 1961.
Chassis included between AR10204*00011 and *00232.

NO SIGNIFICANT MODIFICATIONS TO THE FOLLOWING MODELS:
Giulietta Sprint Veloce (type 750 E). (lightened with sliding windows, including the "Confortevole").
Chassis included between AR1493*05834 and *07968.
1900 Super (type 1483). Chassis included between AR1900*19090 and *19264.
1900 C Super Sprint (2ⁿᵈ version) **(type 1484)**. Chassis included between AR1900C*10564 and *10601.

NO CARS PRODUCED:
Giulietta Promiscua (type 750 C).

GIULIETTA
(TYPE 101.00, ENGINE TYPE AR1315)
4 cylinders in line, 1290 cc, 53 hp, twin overhead camshafts. Wheelbase 2380 mm.

ALFA ROMEO SALOON

The new series of **Giulietta** saloons was introduced in September at the Frankfurt Motor Show and the most obvious aesthetic modifications included the new grills, lights and the modern dashboard design. The bumper bars were those of the previous series.
The engines were modified by placing the mechanical petrol pump in a lower position on the crankcase and fitting a new cylinder head, obviously without the pump itself. The stems of the inlet valves and exhaust went from 8 to 9 mm and the main journal of the drive shaft was increased slightly, making the whole system more robust.
New engine numbers started with AR1315*500006.
Chassis included between AR1488*30001 and *32024.

GIULIETTA t.i.
(TYPE 101.11, ENGINE TYPE AR1315)
4 cylinders in line, 1290 cc, 65 hp, twin overhead camshafts. Wheelbase 2380 mm.

ALFA ROMEO SALOON

The new t.i. was also presented at the Frankfurt Motor Show. Modifications were identical to those carried out on the saloon, except for the newly designed bumper bars which were given rubber guards and bigger rear lights, although their position was the same as the saloon's. The engine was subjected to the same modifications as the saloon; but the car still had its twin choke carburettors and its power output was the same as the previous model. Regardless, the more attentive Alfa enthusiasts did not like the diminished sporting sensation of the new model. The interior was changed from *pied de poule* to a more modest design. Numbering of the new AR 1315 engines began with 800009.
Chassis included between AR1468*20001 and *24007.

GIULIETTA PROMISCUA
(TYPE 101.22, ENGINE TYPE AR1315)
4 cylinders in line, 1290 cc, 53 hp, twin overhead camshafts. Wheelbase 2380 mm.

COLLI STATION WAGON

A lot of 71 vehicles built by Carrozzeria Colli of Milan with the first series engine. Aesthetic modifications were the same as those made to the saloon.

Chassis and engine numbers were included in those of the **Giulietta** saloon.

GIULIETTA SPRINT
(TYPE 101.02, ENGINE TYPE AR1315)

4 cylinders in line, 1290 cc, 80 hp, twin overhead camshafts. Wheelbase 2380 mm.

COUPE'

With the new type 101.02, the **Giulietta Sprint** started out along the road towards definitive configuration. While still retaining the material with vertical stripes, the seat design was modified and never changed after that. During the year, the covering material was re-placed with the definitive "salt and pepper" type. Document pockets in the door panels were still small and set into the panels themselves. With this new series the engine was made more robust, in line with those of the saloon and t.i., by increasing the dimensions of the valve stems and the main journal of the crankshaft; power remained unchanged. Numbering of the new engines start-ed with AR1315*010001. **Chassis included between AR1493*20001 and *21667.**

GIULIETTA SPIDER
(TYPE 101.03, ENGINE TYPE AR1315)

4 cylinders in line, 1290 cc, 80 hp, twin overhead camshafts. Wheelbase 2250 mm.

PININ FARINA ROADSTER

From chassis AR1495*08001, the body shell was lengthened by 5 cm and that, perhaps, penalised the harmony of the car. Naturally, the lengthening required many modifications between the door and the rear wing: new drive-shaft, new soft-top, new hard top, new car-pets were the principal ones. Door windows without glass butterfly windows fixed to the door were discontinued (fitted intermittently from car number AR1495*02208) and the glove-box in the dashboard was given a lockable door. The seats were still smooth, without stitching. The engines were part of a single lot, in common with the **Giulietta Sprint,** and numbered from AR1315*010001. **Chassis included from AR1495*08001 to *08668.**

GIULIETTA SPRINT SPECIALE
(TYPE 101.20, ENGINE TYPE AR00120)

4 cylinders in line, 1290 cc, 100 hp, twin overhead camshafts. Wheelbase 2250 mm.

BERTONE COUPE'

Deliveries began in mid-1959. Light alloy bodies and plexiglass windows were discontinued and replaced with more conventional ones, more suitable to a car no longer being used for motor sport. There were still no bumpers and the boot lid was like that of the first series. AR00120 engines which, some months later, were also fitted to the **Giulietta SZ,** were installed in the first type (higher compression head, 8 mm valve stems, smaller diameter main journals). The two carburettors were still Weber 40 DCO3. **Chassis AR10120*00001, *00003, *00010, *00011, *00013 and from AR10120*00014 to *00101.**

_ GIULIETTA SZ (SPRINT ZAGATO) _
(TYPE 101.26, ENGINE TYPE AR00120)
4 cylinders in line, 1290 cc, 100 hp, twin overhead camshafts. Wheelbase 2250 mm.

ZAGATO COUPE'

Carrozzeria Zagato, which had already built some Alfas with bodies entirely in light alloy - **Giulietta Sprint Veloce** using the floor pan of the **Giulietta Sprint Speciale** - was finally able to create a sensational car. The small coupè was a great success for Alfa Romeo, both in terms of its high performance and its motor sport results. In fact, the SZ would mainly be used for sport. The chassis was the same as that of the Sprint Speciale and the engine belonged to the first type (high compression head, 8 mm valve stems, smaller diameter main journals, two Weber 40 DCO3 carbu-

rettors).
Although production began on 19 December, 1959, (**chassis AR10126*00001**), the presentation

and first deliveries did not take place until the following year.

A pre-production version, still with plexiglass over the headlamps

DAUPHINE
(TYPE AR 1090, ENGINE TYPE R.670-1)
4 cylinders in line, 845 cc, 30 hp, single camshaft in the sump. Wheelbase 2270 mm.

SALOON

In collaboration with Renault, Alfa Romeo assembled and produced some of the bodywork of the **Dauphine**, which was officially presented on 4 June. This car had a 12

volt electrical system instead of the 6 volt French version: seats were covered with the typical *pied-de-poule* material of the **Giulietta t.i. Chassis included between 5192249 and 5525000.**

NO SIGNIFICANT MODIFICATIONS TO THE FOLLOWING MODELS:
Giulietta (type 750 C). Chassis included between AR1488*22445 and *24931.
Giulietta Promiscua (type 750 C). Chassis included in the numbering system of the Giulietta 750 C.
Giulietta t.i. (type 753). Chassis included between AR1468*11178 and *17760.
Giulietta Sprint (type 750 B). Chassis included between AR1493*07737 and *10273.
Giulietta Sprint Veloce (type 750 E). Chassis included between AR1493*07972 and *11051.
Giulietta Spider (type 750 D). Chassis included between AR1495*05640 and *07213 (doors still with and without butterfly windows).
Giulietta Spider Veloce (type 750 F). Chassis included between AR1495*05631 and *07144(doors still with and without butterfly windows).
1900 Super (type 1483). Chassis AR1900*19230, *19238, *19239, *19248, *19252.
2000 (type 102.00). Chassis included between AR10200*00237 and *01174.
2000 Spider (type 102.04). Chassis included between AR10204*00001 and *001185.

1960

GIULIETTA
(TYPE 101.00, ENGINE TYPE AR00100)
4 cylinders in line, 1290 cc, 53 hp, twin overhead camshafts. Wheelbase 2380 mm.

ALFA ROMEO SALOON

The new-type engines with numbers starting from AR00100*03400 were subjected to no technical variation, compared to the previous AR1315 updated in the autumn of 1959. Aesthetics unchanged. **Chassis included between AR*110001 and *111959.**

GIULIETTA t.i.
(TYPE 101.11, ENGINE TYPE AR00111)
4 cylinders in line, 1290 cc, 65 hp, twin overhead camshafts. Wheelbase 2380 mm.

ALFA ROMEO SALOON

The only variation was the change of engine (AR00111) which maintained the technical characteristics of the previous AR1315, updated in the autumn of 1959. General aesthetics unchanged. Engine numbers began with AR00111*06600 and the chassis AR1468*125001. **Chassis included between AR*125001 and *131473.**

GIULIETTA SPRINT
(TYPE 101.02, ENGINE TYPE AR00102)
4 cylinders in line, 1290 cc, 80 hp, twin overhead camshafts. Wheelbase 2380 mm.

BERTONE COUPE'

In common with the **Giulietta Spider,** new-type engines were fitted from number AR*155001 and chassis number AR00102*14300. Around AR*156000, document pockets were enlarged; the edge covered the whole door panel with oblique progression and was kept in place by a central button. The new number plate holder, which required the lights to be located in the wings, was introduced earlier. No other technical or aesthetic variation. **Chassis included between AR*155001 and *158174.**

GIULIETTA SPRINT VELOCE
(TYPE 101.06, ENGINE TYPE AR00106)
4 cylinders in line, 1290 cc, 90 hp, twin overhead camshafts. Wheelbase 2380 mm.

BERTONE COUPE'

With the new series, the aesthetics of the Sprint Veloce and Sprint were unified.
The 80 litre petrol tank, the "long" conic torque (10/41), the rev counter up to 8000 rpm, the speedometer up to 220 km/h and, obviously, the more powerful engine with an updated twin choke horizontal carburettor, the Weber 40 DCOE 2, all remained. The engine was further developed in line with the rest of the range: new design cylinder head, 9 mm valve stems, bigger diameter main journals of the crankshaft.
The 750 E still remained in production.
Chassis included between AR1493*23490 and *25868, and between AR*155114 and *156807.

GIULIETTA SPIDER
(TYPE 101.03, ENGINE TYPE AR00102)

4 cylinders in line, 1290 cc, 80 hp, twin overhead camshafts. Wheelbase 2250 mm.

PININ FARINA ROADSTER

From chassis AR*167001 and AR00102*14300 the Sprint engine was also fitted to the new Spider.

No technical or aesthetic variation. Smooth until this model, the squabs and backrests of the seats were made with parallel stitching from around chassis AR*167800, although this is not confirmed.

Chassis included between AR*167001 and *168732.

GIULIETTA SPIDER VELOCE
(TYPE 750 F, ENGINE TYPE AR00106)

4 cylinders in line, 1290 cc, 90 hp, twin overhead camshafts. Wheelbase 2250 mm.

PININ FARINA ROADSTER

The first AR00106-type new engines were installed in a small lot of

long wheelbase 750 F cars. As happened with the AR1315, these engines, already described in the Sprint Veloce section, would also be fitted in no particular order to the

two versions.
Chassis included between AR1495*09543 and *10601.

GIULIETTA SPIDER VELOCE
(TYPE 101.07, ENGINE TYPE AR00106)

4 cylinders in line, 1290 cc, 90 hp, twin overhead camshafts. Wheelbase 2250 mm.

PININ FARINA ROADSTER

A further evolution of the **Giulietta Spider Veloce** took place with

the new type 101.07 fitted, obviously, with the new AR00106 engine. As with the Spider, the parallel stitching of the seats was introduced, presumably from chassis

AR*167948, but this is unconfirmed.
Chassis included between AR1495*10603 and *11678 and between AR*167075 and *168766.

GIULIETTA SPRINT SPECIALE
(TYPE 101.20, ENGINE TYPE AR00120)
4 cylinders in line, 1290 cc, 100 hp, twin overhead camshafts. Wheelbase 2250 mm.

BERTONE COUPE'

The slow evolution reached the definitive configuration of the Bertone coupè. The front end design was slightly modified compared to the previous year's model, bumpers were fitted and the rear end was modified with a border along the edge of the boot lid, which ended the rear of the car. In common with the Giulietta SZ, the AR00120 engines were part of the first lot (high compression head, 8 mm valve stems, smaller diameter main journals) until AR00120*00200. However, still characterised by the same type AR00120, from number AR00120*00201 the engines were updated to second series specification (new design cylinder head, 9 mm valve stems, bigger diameter main journals). Engine numbers were not of the same progression as those for the chassis.

Chassis: AR10120*00004, *00005, *00007, *00008, and included between AR10120*00103 and *00395.

GIULIETTA SZ (SPRINT ZAGATO)
(TYPE 101.26, ENGINE TYPE AR00120)
4 cylinders in line, 1290 cc, 100 hp, twin overhead camshafts. Wheelbase 2250 mm.

ZAGATO COUPE'

Production began of the new Zagato coupè. Experiments were carried out on front triple brake shoes; the new system called for the transfer of the conventional front brake grouping to the rear axle. All examples of this model are round tailed. The engine was the AR00120 which, except on rare occasions, was part of the first lot (cylinder head with built-in fuel pump, 8mm valve stems, crankshaft with small dimension main journals and Weber 40 DCO3 carburettors).
Compared to the previous year's cars, the plexiglass headlight covers were discontinued and the front lateral slits had shields of three horizontal profiles. Small chrome door handles were also introduced.
Chassis from AR10126*00002 to *00044, *00047, from AR10126*00049 to *00056, from AR10126*00058 to *00066, *00068.

When it was first presented, the car was still fitted with the traditional braking system

---

NO SIGNIFICANT MODIFICATIONS TO THE FOLLOWING MODELS:
Dauphine (type 1090). Chassis included between 5530001 and 5900800.
Giulietta (type 101.00 with engine type AR1315). Chassis included between AR1468*31979 and *35200.
Giulietta Promiscua (type 101.22). Chassis included in the Giulietta (type 101.00) numbering system.
Giulietta t.i. (type 101.11 with engine type AR1315). Chassis included between AR1468*23736 and *34200.
Giulietta Sprint (type 101.02 with engine type AR1315). Chassis included between AR1493*21606 and *26200.
Giulietta Sprint Veloce (type 750 E with engine type AR1315). Chassis included between AR1493*11001 and *11099.
Giulietta Spider (type 101.03) with engine type AR1315. Chassis included between AR1495*08526 and *11900.
Giulietta Spider Veloce (type 750 F with engine AR1315 for the U.S. market, wheelbase 2200 mm), Chassis from AR1495*07501 to *07612.
2000 (type 102.00) Chassis included between AR10200*01013 and *02198 , and between AR10200*100001 and *100126.
2000 Spider (type 102.04). Chassis included between AR10204*01056 and *03198.

1961

ONDINE
(TYPE 1090/A – 1094)

4 cylinders in line, 845 cc, 30 hp, single cam in sump. Wheelbase 2270 mm.

SALOON

Better finished than the **Dauphine,** the car included a number of improvements: disc wheels, rear bumpers with rubber guards, dashboard in non-reflective material, front boot lined with cloth, chromed edges for the rear window, drip moulding and side panels. **Chassis from 1084651 to 11159356.**

2000 SPRINT
(TYPE 102.05, ENGINE TYPE AR00205)

4 cylinders in line, 1975 cc, 115 hp, twin overhead camshafts. Wheelbase 2580 mm.

BERTONE COUPE'

Born as an updated version of the **1900 Super** saloon, the new car was produced by Bertone and designed by a very young Giorgio Giugiaro. Modern and elegant, it completed the **2000** range, which also included a roadster.
Chassis: AR10205*00001, *106709 (prototypes) and included between AR10205*106003 and *106708.

2000 SPIDER
(TYPE 102.04, ENGINE TYPE AR00204)

4 cylinders in line, 1975 cc, 115 hp, twin overhead camshafts. Wheelbase 2500 mm.

TOURING ROADSTER

Carrozzeria Touring, who had produced the open version of the 2000 since 1958, developed a new 2+2 model. Therefore, Alfa Romeo reduced the list price of the first version of the Roadster, which remained in production at Lit 100,000 less.
Chassis between AR*102005 and *102250.

GIULIETTA SPIDER
(TYPE 101.03, ENGINE TYPE AR00102)
4 cylinders in line, 1290 cc, 80 hp, twin overhead camshafts. Wheelbase 2250 mm.

PININFARINA ROADSTER

In July, Alfa Romeo unveiled the latest version of the **Giulietta Spider,** which remained more or less unchanged, including those with the Giulia engine and gearbox. Modifications were made to the tail lights, which also had reflectors for the accommodation of which the rear end was slightly re-designed; a stainless steel border surrounded the hood compartment, which was already present on many examples of the previous version; a new type of boot hinge, which was also fitted with hood attachments; the upper dashboard was padded with a plastic material; a new interior rear vision mirror with dipping device; a cigarette lighter in the dashboard and an ashtray on the transmission tunnel.

No mechanical modifications, except for the substitution of the four-blade cooling fan in aluminium with another with six nylon blades. From 20 December of the previous year, a unification of seat colours was announced, including piping which decorated the stitching and the edges of the mats. Yet, this model was only introduced from car AR*169055, the 169057, 169058, 169059, 169060, 169062 and 169065, all with the previous finish, still maintaining the original colour. From AR*169066, the unification of colours was adopted definitively.

Chassis included between AR*169066 and *171843.

GIULIETTA SPIDER VELOCE
(TYPE 101.07, ENGINE TYPE AR00106)
4 cylinders in line, 1290 cc, 90 hp, twin overhead camshafts. Wheelbase 2250 mm.

PININFARINA ROADSTER

This model received the same bodywork update as the Spider, since the body shells were taken from the same lot from the beginning of production

The mechanical characteristics remained unchanged. The radiator fan remained in aluminium.

Chassis included between AR*169230 and *170818.

_ GIULIETTA SZ (SPRINT ZAGATO) _
(TYPE 101.26, ENGINE TYPE AR00120)

4 cylinders in line, 1290 cc, 100 hp, twin overhead camshafts. Wheelbase 2250 mm.

ZAGATO (ROUND-TAILED) COUPE'

Almost all versions made in 1961 were given new engines of the AR00120 type, with re-designed cylinder head and crankshaft with bigger diameter main journals, which had been used for some time for the whole range. The carburettors were Weber 40 DCOE2, identical to those fitted to single feed models.

On some cars, the cover of the glove box was eliminated and on others the dash was in glass fibre reinforced plastic instead of aluminium. No aesthetic changes.

The numbering system of the new engines began with AR00120*00201.

Chassis AR10126*00045, *00046, *00057, *00067, from AR10126*00069 to *00169, *00171.

_ GIULIETTA SZ (SPRINT ZAGATO) _
(TYPE 101.26, ENGINE TYPE AR00120)

4 cylinders in line, 1290 cc, 100 hp, twin overhead camshafts. Wheelbase 2250 mm.

ZAGATO (SHORT-TAILED) COUPE'

In collaboration with the Servizio Esperienze Speciale (test department) and with the fundamental support of Ercole Spada, a newly employed young designer, Carrozzeria Zagato produced the short-tailed version of the **Giulietta SZ,** using the results of aerodynamic studies by Kamm. The new car was lower, the headlights were given plexiglass covers, the windscreen and windows were newly designed and the tail was similar to that of the **Giulia TZ.**

There were no mechanical changes; the all-new engine, with the new-design cylinder head and bigger diameter main journals, were used from AR00120*00201 onwards and also fitted to the Sprint Speciale but they were almost always modified, because, of the 44 made up until 1963, few were used as touring cars. Girling disc brakes were introduced on this model after considerable testing on experimental vehicle AR10126*00047 used by the Servizio Esperienze, but only on the front wheels, while the rear wheels continued to be fitted with modified front group drums. On request, disc brakes were also fitted to the Round Tail if used for sport.

Chassis AR10126*00170, *00172, *00173, *00174, *00175.

GIULIETTA
(TYPE 101.28, ENGINE TYPE AR00128)
4 cylinders in line, 1290 cc, 62 hp, twin overhead camshafts. Wheelbase 2380 mm.

ALFA ROMEO SALOON

Alfa Romeo presented the new saloon in the autumn at the Frankfurt Motor Show: the power of the ordinary version was increased by 9 hp, raising the car's top speed to 145 km/h. Aesthetically, the three front air intakes were covered with a Sprint-type grille, the bonnet and boot lid were bigger (the step which defined the lower part was eliminated), while the bumpers were those of the previous model. The lateral repeater was moved further forward, nearer the headlamp insert. The six-blade nylon fan was also introduced.
Chassis included between AR*300001 and *303583.

GIULIETTA t.i.
(TYPE 101.29, ENGINE TYPE AR00129)
4 cylinders in line, 1290 cc, 74 hp, twin overhead camshafts. Wheelbase 2380 mm.

ALFA ROMEO SALOON

The t.i. also made its debut at Frankfurt: the 74 hp of the new AR00129-type engine gave the car a top speed of 155 km/h. The six-blade nylon fan was adopted, the carburettor was substituted by the Solex C32 PAIA-5. The aesthetic modifications are those made to the saloon, but the bumpers, even if of more modern design, were also used for the previous version. The front seats were separate and the seat backs reclinable, on their backs were net pockets. Seat coverings were changed to damask material. On request, the car was supplied with a floor-mounted gear lever.

Chassis included between AR*200001 and *207708.

NO SIGNIFICANT MOIDFICATIONS TO THESE MODELS:
Dauphine (type 1090). Chassis included between 5923601 and 6031150.
Giulietta (type 101.00). Chassis included between AR*111922 and *115140.
Giulietta t.i. (type 101.11). Chassis included between AR*131243 and *143725.
Giulietta Sprint (type 101.02). Chassis included between AR*158175 and *162309.
Giulietta Sprint Veloce (type 101.06). Chassis included between AR*156329 and *162238.
Giulietta Spider (type 101.03). (1960 version). Chassis included between AR*168733 and *169065.
Giulietta Spider Veloce (type 101.07). (1960 version). Chassis included between AR*168741 and *169023.
Giulietta Sprint Speciale (type 101.20). Chassis AR10120*00173, *00233, *00250, *00254, *00257, *00261, *00264, *00266, *00267, *00272, *00274, *00278, *00279, *00282, *00284, *00288; included between AR10120*00290 and *00750; included between AR*177001 and *177310. preceededing AR10120
2000 (type 102.00). Chassis included between AR10200*02039 and *02200 and included between AR10200*100005 and *100701.
2000 Spider (type 102.04). Chassis included between AR10204*02735 and *03200.

GIULIETTA t.i.
(TYPE 101.29, ENGINE TYPE AR00129)

4 cylinders in line, 1290 cc, 74 hp, twin overhead camshafts. Wheelbase 2380 mm.

ALFA ROMEO SALOON

At the beginning of the year, the t.i. was switched completely to a floor-mounted gear lever to satisfy customers who wanted a more sporting drive, in keeping with the small Alfa. It should be noted that the modification was made a year earlier for the British market. Apart from that, the car's characteristics remained unchanged. **Chassis included between AR*207036 and *221600.**

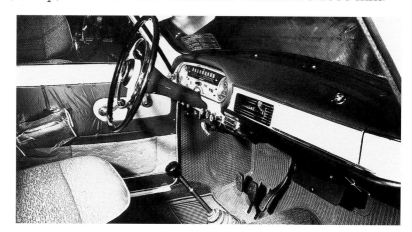

2600
(TYPE 106.00, ENGINE TYPE AR00600)

6 cylinders in line, 2584 cc, 130 hp, twin overhead camshafts. Wheelbase 2720 mm.

ALFA ROMEO SALOON

An evolution of the **2000,** of which it conserved a slightly updated body. The new and very powerful six cylinder engine ended criticism attracted by the old engine that it was too closely related to the old **1900.** Two Solex 32 PAIA4 carburettors. **Chassis included between AR*800001 and *800739.** The right-hand drive **2600** (type 106.07). **Chassis: AR*850001, *850002.**

2600 SPRINT
(TYPE 106.02, ENGINE TYPE AR00601)

6 cylinders in line, 2584 cc, 145 hp, twin overhead camshafts. Wheelbase 2580 mm.

BERTONE COUPE'

The successful design of the **2000 Sprint** by Giorgio Giugiaro was also used for this new six cylinder model: this version hads three Solex 44 PHH carburettors. Carrozzeria Bertone built the new coupè which, like the saloon, boasted a new and much more powerful engine. **Chassis included between AR*820001 and *821396.**

2600 SPIDER
(TYPE 106.01, ENGINE TYPE AR00601)

6 cylinders in line, 2584 cc, 145 hp, twin overhead camshafts. Wheelbase 2500 mm.

TOURING ROADSTER

Carrozzeria Touring also produced the roadster version of the new **2600**. The characteristics of the previous **2000** remained almost unchanged and the company limited itself to a slight re-styling, eliminating part of the side slats. In addition, the bumper bars became mono units and just one air intake was built into the bonnet. The mechanics were the same as the Sprint. **Chassis included between AR*191004 and *191698.**

GIULIA T.I.
(TYPE 105.14, ENGINE TYPE AR00514)

4 cylinders in line, 1570 cc, 92 hp, twin overhead camshafts. Wheelbase 2510 mm.

ALFA ROMEO SALOON

This modern new Alfa Romeo saloon retained the best of the **Giulietta,** including an engine of identical 'architecture' distinguished, however, by an oil dip stick in the crankcase; the gearbox was five-speed; the front brakes were three shoe; the rear axle was re-designed, particularly the anchorage units of the body shell, but it maintained the characteristics of the **Giulietta.**

It was a highly successful car, in particular because of its high performance, the extremely successful body design research carried out by the company to create an impact-absorbing body: front and rear ends were highly deformable, while the cockpit was of very solid construction. It was one of the safest cars available. **Chassis included between AR*400002 and *407354.**

GIULIA SPRINT
(TYPE 101.12, ENGINE TYPE AR00112)

4 cylinders in line, 1570 cc, 92 hp, twin overhead camshafts. Wheelbase 2380 mm

BERTONE COUPE'

While maintaining the appearance of the **Giulietta Sprint,** the car was given a new 1570 cc engine. Its power output was the same as the **Giulia T.I.** but the engine maintained the aesthetic characteristics of the **Giulietta,** in particular the oil dip stick, which was not in the crankcase but in the sump. Like the **Giulia T.I.,** the front brakes were three shoe, extensively tested on the **Giulietta SZ,** and the gearbox was five-speed. The graphically updated instruments were placed horizontally, the rev counter climbing to 8000 rpm and the speedometer 220 km/h. The door panels were completely covered in imitation leather. **Chassis included between AR*352001 and *355824.**

GIULIA SPIDER

(TYPE 101.23, ENGINE TYPE AR00112)

4 cylinders in line, 1570 cc, 92 hp, twin overhead camshafts. Wheelbase 2250 mm.

PININFARINA ROADSTER

Identical mechanical characteristics to the **Giulia Sprint**. As well as the modifications carried out on the **Giulietta Spider** in July, 1961, other changes included: a decorative air intake for the bonnet with chrome edged surround, necessary to house the taller engine; 1600 script on the boot lid.
Chassis included between AR*372001 and *375175.

R4 SALOON – R4 LIMOUSINE

(TYPE 1123)

4 cylinders in line, 845 cc, 27 hp, single camshaft in sump.
Right wheelbase 2440 mm, left 2400 mm.

SALOON

In line with the agreement with

Renault, Alfa Romeo also built the R4. It was made only in white.
Chassis numbers not available.

NO SIGNIFICANT MODIFICATIONS TO THE FOLLOWING MODELS:
Dauphine (type 1090). Chassis included between 6080601 and 6113760.
Ondine (type 1090-type 1094). Chassis included between 1100076 and 1159356.
Giulietta (type 101.28). Chassis included between AR*300001 and *303900.
Giulietta Sprint (type 101.02). Chassis from AR*162310 to *162691 and from AR*350001 to *350975
Giulietta Sprint Veloce (type 101.06). Chassis included between AR*162071 and *162212 and between AR*350232 and *350961.
Giulietta Spider (type 101.03). Chassis included between AR*171629 and *171849 and between AR*370001 and *371089.
Giulietta Spider Veloce (type 101.07). Chassis: AR*171715, from AR*171850 to *171903, *370004, *370005, *370009, *370010, *370012, *370013, *370016.
Giulietta Sprint Speciale (type 101.20). Chassis: AR10120*00376, AR*177240, *177269, *177273, *177284, *177294, *177296, *177298, *177300, *177301, *177302, *177307; and from AR*177311 to *177508.
Giulietta SZ (type 101.26) (short-tailed). Chassis from AR10126*00176 to *00198 (except AR10126*00178 and *00179 not produced and AR10126*00189 produced in 1963).
2000 (type 102.00). Chassis included between AR10200*100552 and *100727.
2000 Sprint (type 102.05). Chassis included between AR10205*106608 and *106708.

GIULIA SPRINT SPECIALE
(TYPE 101.21, ENGINE TYPE AR00121)

4 cylinders in line, 1570 cc, 112 hp, twin overhead camshafts. Wheelbase 2250 mm.

BERTONE COUPE'

The sports saloon with the new, more flexible 1600 cc engine was unveiled at the 1963 Geneva Motor Show. The top speed (200 km/h) was that of the **Giulietta Sprint Speciale**.
Compared to the Sprint Speciale, the body and interior were slightly updated and the car took on the appearance of a real and comfortable grand tourer.
Chassis included between AR*380002 and *380794.

GIULIA T.I. SUPER
(TYPE 105.16, ENGINE TYPE AR00516)

4 cylinders in line, 1570 cc, 112 hp, twin overhead camshafts. Wheelbase 2510 mm.

ALFA ROMEO SALOON

The racing version of the **Giulia T.I.** was presented at Monza on 24 April, 1963. The higher performance was obtained with an engine identical to that of the **Giulia SS**. The gear lever was floor-mounted, the wheels light alloy (*elektron*), the car had oval windows like those of the **Giulietta**; yet some examples were fitted with the same type of wheel but with parallelogram-shaped windows. The seats were the sporting, retentive type. Disc brakes were fitted to all four wheels, although many retained the drum brake system.
Chassis: AR*595001, from AR*595003 to *595181 (except AR*595055 not produced, except AR*595019, *595065, *595127, *595138, *595139, *595150, *595151, *595156, *595167, *595175, *595178 produced in 1964 and except AR*595169 which was demolished), AR*595183, *595186, *595190, *595194, *595196, *595201, *595202, *595203, *595205, *595210, *595212, *595219, *595236.

GIULIA T.I.
(TYPE 105.14, ENGINE TYPE AR00514)

4 cylinders in line, 1570 cc, 92 hp, twin overhead camshafts. Wheelbase 2510.

ALFA ROMEO SALOON

In August from chassis AR*422001 to AR*422040 and from AR*423501 onwards, disc brakes were fitted to all four wheels. The appearance remained unchanged.

Chassis from AR*407355 to *422043 and AR*423501 to*434181.

GIULIA SPRINT GT
(TYPE 105.02, ENGINE TYPE AR00502)

4 cylinders in line, 1570 cc, 106 hp, twin overhead camshafts. Wheelbase 2350 mm.

BERTONE COUPE'

To design this new coupè, Carrozzeria Bertone collaborated with the young Giorgio Giugiaro.
Destined to become a worthy substitute the old **Giulia Sprint**, the GT was presented to the press on 9 September, 1963, and then at the Frankfurt Motor Show.

The mechanics were those of the **Giulia T.I.**, the engine fed by two Weber 40 DCOE4 carburettors, disc brakes all round. The **Giulia Sprint GT** was the first model to be built in the new Arese factory, with the exception of some mechanical parts which were still supplied by Portello.
Chassis from AR*600001 to *600951.

1300 SPRINT
(TYPE 101.02, ENGINE TYPE AR00102)

4 cylinders in line, 1290 cc, 80 hp, twin overhead camshafts. Wheelbase 2380 mm..

BERTONE COUPE'

After a long break, the **Giulietta Sprint** went back into production but no longer with that name, as the tendency was towards the Giulia range and to cut all ties with the old models.
While retaining the old designation (type 101.02 and engine AR00102) for homologation reasons, the new car had front disc brakes and the round instruments were arranged like those of the **Giulia Sprint**, as was the interior.
Chassis included between AR*384001 and *384439.

GIULIA TZ
(TYPE 105.11, ENGINE TYPE AR00511)
4 cylinders in line, 1570 cc, 112 hp, twin overhead camshafts. Wheelbase 2200 mm.

ZAGATO COUPE'

After the first unofficial G.T.Z. (Gran Turismo Zagato) denomination, the model assumed the designation **Giulia TZ** (Tubolare Zagato or Tubular Zagato) as the chassis was made of small diameter steel tubing, which differentiated it profoundly from the normal production Giulia. The unusual rear axle with independent wheels, brakes at the exit of the differential and trailing half-axles were innovative, as was the utilisation of *elektron,* a very light alloy used almost exclusively for racing cars since the Thirties, with which to make some components and the wheels, identical to those of the **Giulia T.I. Super**. The gestation of the TZ was long, but the car relaunched the sporting image of Alfa Romeo, which was so close to the heart of company president Giuseppe Luraghi. Engine, gearbox and a number of other components came from the Giulia, while the remaining parts were designed and made at Portello and supplied to Autodelta at Udine, where the car was built under the direction of Ing. Carlo Chiti.
Chassis: AR10511*750002, *750004, *750005, *750007, *750022, *750025, *750029.

NO SIGNIFICANT MODIFICATIONS TO THE FOLLOWING MODELS:
Dauphine (type 1090). Chassis included between 6116153 and 6200975 and from 0510008 and 0529805.
Giulietta (type 101.28). Chassis in 1962 numbering system.
Giulietta t.i. (type 101.29). Chassis included between AR*221601 and *233631.
Giulietta SZ (type 101.26). Only one car produced: chassis AR10126*00189.
Giulia Sprint (type 101.12). Chassis included between AR*355718 and *359000.
Giulia Spider (type 101.23). Chassis included between AR*375024 and *378730.
Giulia Spider right hand drive (type 101.19). Chassis from AR*383001 to *383404.
2600 (type 106.00). Chassis included between AR*800575 and *801185.
2600 Spider (type 106.01). Chassis included between AR*191039 and *192861.
2600 Sprint (type 106.02). Chassis included between AR*821258 and *824225.

1964

GIULIA 1300
(TYPE 105.06, ENGINE TYPE AR00506)

4 cylinders in line, 1290 cc, 78 hp, twin overhead camshafts. Wheelbase 2510 mm.

ALFA ROMEO SALOON

The official presentation of the Giulia 1300, which substituted the **Giulietta**, took place on 11 May at Monza. The radiator grill was simplified to include two headlights and the fittings in general were more sober. The gearbox was four-speed. The engine, similar to the AR00129 of the **Giulietta**, was given more power and achieved a high degree of reliability. **Chassis from AR*550004 to AR*562022.**

GIULIA SPIDER VELOCE
(TYPE 101.18, ENGINE TYPE AR00121)

4 cylinders in line, 1570 cc, 112 hp, twin overhead camshafts. Wheelbase 2250 mm.

PININFARINA ROADSTER

This car was unveiled at the same time as the **Giulia 1300** and the **Giulia T.I.** and had a floor-mounted gear lever. The engine was identical to that of the **Giulia Sprint Speciale** even in its designation (AR00121).

The general technical characteristics were the same as those of the front disc brake version of the **Giulia Sprint Speciale**. Its appearance differed from the **Giulia Spider** in that its 1600 script was on the boot lid. **Chassis included between AR*390001 and *390300.**

GIULIA GTC
(TYPE 105.25, ENGINE TYPE AR00502)

4 cylinders in line, 1570 cc, 106 hp, twin overhead camshafts. Wheelbase 2350 mm.

BERTONE/TOURING CABRIOLET

The **Giulia Gran Turismo Cabriolet** had the same technical characteristics and performance as the Sprint GT. The body was built by Carrozzeria Touring of Milan. The platform was specially reinforced to reduce flexing caused by the lack of a roof panel, but further strengthening was introduced after the first examples were built. **Chassis included between AR*755020 and *755241.**

GIULIA T.I.
(TYPE 105.08, ENGINE TYPE AR00514)
4 cylinders in line, 1570 cc, 92 hp, twin overhead camshafts. Wheelbase 2510 mm.

ALFA ROMEO SALOON

The **Giulia T.I.** with its steering column gear-change and front bench seat, was joined in May by a version with a floor-mounted gear lever and bucket front seats, which were optional on the standard version.
The mechanics were unchanged, although disc brakes were on all four wheels.
Chassis from AR*442711 to *453459.

2600
(TYPE 106.00, ENGINE TYPE AR00600)
6 cylinders in line, 2584 cc, 130 hp, twin overhead camshafts. Wheelbase 2720 mm.

ALFA ROMEO SALOON

The updated version of the top-of-the-range 2600 saloon was unveiled at the 1964 Turin Motor Show. The chrome edging on the sides had been eliminated and the lateral directional indicators were of new design. An electric clock was added and the rear vision mirror was in the centre above the windscreen. The front seats were separate with body-hugging backs and the rears were of new design. Disc brakes on all four wheels. The remaining mechanical parts were unchanged.
Chassis included between AR*801186 and AR*8801290 (including examples of the first version).
2600 with right hand drive (type 106.07).
Chassis from AR*850305 to *850402 including the cars produced in 1965.

NO SIGNIFICANT MODIFICATIONS TO THE FOLLOWING MODELS:
Dauphine (type 1090). Chassis included between 0529806 and 0562262.
Giulietta t.i. (type 101.29). Chassis included between AR*232808 and *238756.
1300 Sprint (type 101.02). Chassis included between AR*384206 and *385713.
Giulia T.I. (type 105.14). Chassis from AR*434182 to *442710.
Giulia T.I. Super (type 105.16). Chassis: AR*595019, *595065, *595127, 595138, *595139, *595150, *595151, *595156, *595167, *595175, *595178, from AR*595182 to *595509 (except AR*595183, *595186, *595190, *595194, *595196, *595201, *595202, *595203, *595205, *595210, *595212, *595219, *595236 produced in 1963 and excluding *595245, *595397, *595414 which were not produced).
Giulia Spider (type 101.23). Chassis from AR*378731 to *379999, from AR*392001 to *392608.
Giulia Sprint GT (type 105.02). Chassis from AR*600952 to *610776.
Giulia Sprint Speciale (type 101.21). Chassis included between AR*380007 and *381350.
Giulia TZ (type 105.11). Chassis: AR10511*750001, *750003, *750006, from AR10511*750008 to *750020, *750022, *750023, *750026, *750028; from AR10511*750030 to *750033, *750035, *750037, *750038, *750040, from AR10511*750045 to *750048, *750050, *750053; from AR10511*750055 to *750057; from AR10511*750059 to *750068, *750070, *750071; from AR10511*750082 to *750084, *750086, *750094, *750095.
2600 Spider (type 106.01). Chassis included between AR*192188 and *193116.
2600 Sprint (type 106.02). Chassis included between AR*820020 and *826314.
2600 Sprint with right hand drive **(type 106.09).** Chassis from AR*854001 to *854597, including those made in 1965 and 1966.

GIULIA SPRINT GTA

(TYPE 105.32 STUDY CODE – TYPE 105.02/TO HOMOLOGATION CODE I.G.M., ENGINE TYPE AR00502/A, OR AROO532/A)

4 cylinders in line, 1570 cc, 115 hp, twin overhead camshafts. Wheelbase 2350 mm.

BERTONE COUPE'

The Giulia Sprint Gran Turismo Alleggerita (lightened) was the name of the new coupè which was created by the company in particular for competition, as it had to take the place of the by then uncompetitive **Giulia T.I. Super** in the touring car category. The body was made from *peraluman*, an extremely light aluminum, zinc and manganese-based alloy which, together with the use of *elektron* for some mechanical parts including the wheels, ensured a 200 kg weight reduction compared to the normal Sprint GT.
But the sensational aspect of this mass-produced car was the cylinder head, which had double ignition (two spark plugs per cylinder). Exploiting the racing rules, the car had four small seats which were just big enough; it competed with great success in the touring car category until 1970, after which it moved on to Gran Turismo and continued racing until almost 1980.
Chassis included between AR*613001 and *613917.

Giulia Sprint GTA right hand drive (type 105.34).
Chassis included between AR*752501 and AR*753552.

GIULIA SUPER

(TYPE 105.26, ENGINE TYPE AR00526)

4 cylinders in line, 1570 cc, 98 hp, twin overhead camshafts. Wheelbase 2510 mm.

ALFA ROMEO SALOON

The **Giulia Super** resulted from tests carried out on the T.I. Super. With this car, twin-choke carburettors appeared on a saloon car for the first time and provided very high performance with low fuel consumption in a car which could be driven by anyone.
Chassis from AR*305001 to *325783.

GIULIA 1300 T.I.
(TYPE 105.39, ENGINE TYPE AR00539)

4 cylinders in line, 1290 cc, 82 hp, twin overhead camshafts. Wheelbase 2510 mm.

ALFA ROMEO SALOON

The performance of the **Giulia 1300** was increased with the adoption of the five-speed gearbox and a differential with shortened conic torque (8/41).
All of which produced better

acceleration and use of the engine's power. Still only one carburettor (Solex C32 PAIA7) but an increased compression ratio took the car's power to 82 hp without varying the engine revs, which remained at 6000 rpm/1'.
Chassis from AR*575386 to *576263.

GRAN SPORT QUATTRORUOTE
(TYPE 101.23, ENGINE TYPE AR00112)

4 cylinders in line, 1570 cc, 92 hp, twin overhead camshafts. Wheelbase 2600 mm.

ZAGATO ROADSTER

These were the years of the re-evaluation of vintage cars. The Italian motoring magazine Quattroruote convinced Alfa Romeo to build a car which vaguely resembled the **6C 1750 Gran Sport** (1930/33), but with modern technical characteristics.
The car was commissioned from Carrozzeria Zagato, the same

company that built the mythical original Alfa thirty years earlier.
The platform belonged to the **Giulia Spider**, adapted and lengthened.
The engines, the identification code and parameters of which were identical to that of the **Giulia Spider** and **Giulia Sprint**, were included in the numbering systems of those cars.
Only two cars were built in 1965.
Chassis: AR*393002, *393003.

GIULIA SPRINT GT VELOCE
(TYPE 105.36, ENGINE TYPE AR00536)

4 cylinders in line, 1570 cc, 109 hp, twin overhead camshafts. Wheelbase 2350 mm.

BERTONE COUPE'

Perhaps the optimum results of the GTA had some influence on the creation of the GT Veloce. Although not considerable, the increase in power output (3 hp compared to the GT) still offered greater driving vivacity. While conserving the same instruments as the GT, the dashboard was covered in imitation wood; the steering wheel was

slightly reduced in size, the seats of excellent design had body-hugging backs and a central panel in imitation woven material. The Veloce script was applied to the right rear between the number plate and the tail light. The radiator grill had three horizontal bars in stainless steel and at the base of the rear pillar was a four-leaf clover emblem.
Chassis: AR*240001, *240002, from AR*240306 to *241106.

2600 SZ

(TYPE 106.12, ENGINE TYPE AR00612)

6 cylinders in line, 2584 cc, 145 hp, twin overhead camshafts. Wheelbase 2500 mm.

ZAGATO COUPE'

This model, presented at the 1965 Frankfurt Motor Show, was the definitive version of this Zagato coupè, but it was a pre-series car embodying a number of similarities to the **Giulia TZ** prototype which was first seen in 1963. The mechanics were the same as the sports version of the **2600** but the wheelbase was of the shorter Spider.
The body was all-steel, a fairly new solution for Zagato, but was not of sufficiently sporting appearance, to the point that the dashboard and glovebox were covered in wood of a rather popular design.

Chassis: AR*856001, *856003, from AR*856005 to *856035.

2600 SPRINT

(TYPE 106.02, ENGINE TYPE AR00601)

6 cylinders in line, 2584 cc, 145 hp, twin overhead camshafts. Wheelbase 2580 mm.

BERTONE COUPE'

The dashboard was updated and covered in wood with air vents placed differently. Seats only in leather with modifications to the panels and related arm rests. The bonnet was given a more effective anti-heat lining. The mechanics remained more or less unchanged. Modifications officially began with chassis AR*825101, but this is contradicted by the production registers.
Chassis included between AR*824170 and *826332.
2600 Sprint right hand drive (type 106.09). **Chassis from AR*854001 to *854597, including cars produced in 1964 and 1966.**

2600 DE LUXE
(TYPE 106.16, ENGINE TYPE AR00600)

6 cylinders in line, 2584 cc, 130 hp, twin overhead camshafts. Wheelbase 2720 mm.

OSI SALOON

OSI (Officina Stampaggi Industriali) made a small series of elegant **2600** cars, using the mechanics of the company saloon.
Chassis from AR*395001 to *395052 (including those produced in 1966).

NO SIGNIFICANT MODIFICATIONS TO THE FOLLOWING MODELS:

Giulietta t.i. (type 101.29). Only one car produced: chassis AR*238757 destined for the Alfa museum.
1300 Sprint (type 101.02). Chassis included between AR*385658 and *386000.
Giulia 1300 (type 105.06). Chassis from AR*562023 to *575385.
Giulia T.I. (type 105.08). Chassis from AR*453460 to *462549.
Giulia Spider (type 101.23). Chassis from AR*392609 to *392852.
Giulia Spider Veloce (type 101.18) Chassis: AR*390267, *390283, *390287, *390290, between AR*390294 and *391092.
Giulia Sprint Speciale (type 101.21). Chassis included between AR*380443 and *381360.
Giulia Sprint GT (type 105.02). Chassis included between AR*610777 and *620839.
Giulia GTC (type 105.25). Chassis included between AR*755002 and *755707.
Giulia GTC right hand drive **(type 105.29).** Chassis from AR*760002 to *760101, including those produced in 1966.
Giulia TZ (type 105.11). Chassis: AR10511*750027, *750034, *750036, *750039; from AR10511*750041 to *750044, *750049, *750054, *750058, *750069; from AR10511*750073 to *750078, *750080, *750081, *750085; from AR10511*750087 to *750092; from AR10511*750096 to *750100, *750102, *750103, *750105.
2600 (type 106.00). Chassis included between AR*801217 and *801701.
2600 right hand drive **(type 106.07).** Chassis from AR*850305 to *850402 including those produced in 1964.
2600 Sprint (type 106.02) (1 only). Chassis included in those of the 2nd version.
2600 Spider (type 106.01). Chassis included between AR*193020 and *193161.

NO CARS PRODUCED:
Giulia T.I. (type 105.14).

COMPETITION CAR NOT FOR PUBLIC SALE
GIULIA TZ 2 (TYPE 105.11) - SPORTING SALOON FOR ROAD AND TRACK RACING

1966

1600 SPIDER (DUETTO)
(TYPE 105.03, ENGINE TYPE AR00536)
4 cylinders in line, 1570 cc, 109 hp, twin overhead camshafts. Wheelbase 2250 mm.

PININFARINA ROADSTER

The new car took the place of the **Giulia Spider,** which was no longer adequate, but still with the body of the **Giulietta**. It was the last Alfa to be designed by Battista Pininfarina, nicknamed Pinin. Alfa Romeo held a competition to find a new name for the car and Duetto was the result. This name was never adopted officially; the company preferred to call it the **1600 Spider.** The mechanics and particularly the engine had the same characteristics as the **Giulia Sprint GT Veloce. Chassis included between AR*660008 and *663298.**

First version with hard top.

GIULIA T.I.
(TYPE 105.08, ENGINE TYPE AR00514)
4 cylinders in line, 1570 cc, 92 hp, twin overhead camshafts. Wheelbase 2510 mm.

ALFA ROMEO SALOON

The improvements made to the **Giulia Super** and **Giulia 1300 T.I.** were also made, in part, to the **Giulia T.I.** with a centrally placed gear lever (the version with a steering column gear change was almost out of production).
It was also given circular instrument dials, a new steering wheel like that of the 1300 T.I., new seating material with the addition of a rear central armrest and stainless steel bumpers.
Chassis from AR*462550 to *467351.

GT 1300 JUNIOR
(TYPE 105.30, ENGINE TYPE AR00530)
4 cylinders in line, 1290 cc, 89 hp, twin overhead camshafts. Wheelbase 2350 mm.

BERTONE COUPE'

Even if dated, the unchanged 1300 cc engine of the **Giulietta** revealed itself extremely suitable for the new GT. And that made the car more accessible to a larger public; it quickly became known as the sports

car for the young.
The dashboard was identical to that of the Sprint GT Veloce and the radiator grill was given just one horizontal bar.
Chassis from AR*1200101 to *1203368.

2600 DE LUXE
(TYPE 106.16, ENGINE TYPE AR00601)
6 cylinders in line, 2584 cc, 130 hp, twin overhead camshafts. Wheelbase 2720 mm.

OSI SALOON

The engine was replaced by that of the Spider and Sprint. Engine power increased 15 hp and improved performance considerably. No other changes.
Chassis included in 1965 numbers.

OSI saloon.

NO SIGNIFICANT MODIFICATIONS TO THE FOLLOWING MODELS:

Giulia 1300 (type 105.06). Chassis included between AR*586898 and *626968.
Giulia 1300 T.I. (type 105.39). Chassis included between AR*576264 and *594999.
Giulia 1300 T.I. right hand drive **(type 105.40).** Chassis from AR*762001 to *762262
Giulia Super (type 105.26). Chassis from AR*325784 to *339976.
Giulia Sprint GT (type 105.02). Chassis included between AR*620284 and *620815.
Giulia GTC (type 105.25). Chassis included between AR*755003 and *775905.
Giulia GTC right hand drive **(type 105.29).** Chassis from AR*760002 to *760101, including those produced in 1965.
Giulia TZ (type 105.11). Chassis; AR10511*750093.
Giulia Sprint GT Veloce (type 105.36). Chassis from AR*240003 to *240305, from AR*241107 to *246946.
Giulia Sprint GT Veloce right hand drive **(type 105.37).** Chassis from AR*298001 to *298778.
Giulia Sprint GTA (type 105.32 - 105.02/A). Chassis included between AR*613853 and *613997.
Giulia Sprint GTA right hand drive **(type 105.34).** Chassis included between AR*753563 and *753778.
Gran Sport Quattroruote (type 101.23). Chassis included between AR*393018 and *393910.
2600 (type 106.00). Chassis from AR*801520 to *801580.
2600 Sprint (type 106.02). Chassis included between AR*825602 and *826409.
2600 Sprint right hand drive **(type 106.09).** Chassis from AR*854001 to *854597, including those produced in 1964 and 1965.
2600 SZ (type 106.12). Chassis included between AR*856036 and *856091.

NO CARS PRODUCED:
Giulia T.I. (type 105.14).

COMPETITION CAR NOT FOR PUBLIC SALE
GIULIA TZ 2 (TYPE 105.11) - SPORTS SALOON FOR ROAD AND TRACK RACING

GIULIA 1300

(TYPE 105.06, ENGINE TYPE AR00506)

4 cylinders in line, 1290 cc, 78 hp, twin overhead camshafts. Wheelbase 2510 mm.

ALFA ROMEO SALOON

The 1967 version was given a new black, fine mesh radiator grill with five horizontal bars in stainless steel. The steering wheel was replaced with that of the GT and the seating was updated. Technical characteristics were unchanged.

Chassis included between AR*626924 and *646940, including the Giulia 1300 T.I. version.

GIULIA 1300 T.I.

(TYPE 105.39, ENGINE TYPE AR00539)

4 cylinders in line, 1290 cc, 82 hp, twin overhead camshafts. Wheelbase 2510 mm.

ALFA ROMEO SALOON

A number of improvements included a brake servo, a dashboard in imitation wood with circular dialled instruments and a new black fine mesh front grill with three horizontal bars in stainless steel. The interior air vents at the base of the windscreen were replaced. The power of the engine, which still had just one Solex C32 PAIA 7 carburettor, remained unchanged. **Chassis included between AR*626855 and *656596, (including the Giulia 1300 version).** **Giulia 1300 T.I.** right hand drive (type 105.40). **Chassis from AR*762263 to *763181.**

GT 1300 JUNIOR

(TYPE 105.30, ENGINE TYPE AR00530)

4 cylinders in line, 1290 cc, 89 hp, twin overhead camshafts. Wheelbase 2350 mm.

BERTONE COUPE'

The variations introduced during the course of the year included a brake servo and the new two-spoke steering wheel.
No other mechanical or aesthetic changes.
Chassis from AR*1203369 to *1215519.
GT 1300 Junior right hand drive (type 105.31).
Chassis from AR*1290001 to *1290633.

GIULIA SUPER
(TYPE 105.26, ENGINE TYPE AR00526)

4 cylinders in line, 1570 cc, 98 hp, twin overhead camshafts. Wheelbase 2510 mm.

ALFA ROMEO SALOON

A black mesh grill for the **Giulia Super** but with five horizontal bars in stainless steel. The steering wheel came from the GT and the seating was updated. The mechanics remained unchanged.
Chassis from AR*859001 to *860638, from AR*862001 to *869597.

1600 SPIDER (DUETTO)
(TYPE 105.03, ENGINE TYPE AR00536)

4 cylinders in line, 1570 cc, 109 hp, twin overhead camshafts. Wheelbase 2250 mm.

PININFARINA ROADSTER

Chassis from AR*663299 to *663961.

The only modification was the introduction of a brake servo. The rest remained unchanged. During the year, production was stopped in readiness for the new **1750 Spider Veloce**.

GRAN SPORT QUATTRORUOTE
(TYPE 101.23, ENGINE TYPE AR00112)

4 cylinders in line. 1570 cc, 92 hp, twin overhead camshafts. Wheelbase 2600 mm.

ZAGATO ROADSTER

A small lot of 10 right hand drive cars was produced for the British market. Both the chassis (101.23) and engine (AR00112) were unchanged.
Chassis from AR*393901 to *393910.

33 STRADALE
(TYPE 105.33, ENGINE TYPE AR00533)
90° V8, 1995 cc, 230 hp, 4 overhead camshafts (2 per main bearing). Wheelbase 2350 mm.

SCAGLIONE/MARAZZI COUPE'

This is the car which, more than any other, probably made Franco Scaglione famous, also because the inspired Florentine designer created the car himself with the help of Autodelta, which supplied the chassis, and Carrozzeria Marazzi, which provided the work force.

A programme imposed by Alfa Romeo decreed that the car's performance should not be less than 95% of their 33 Sport 2 liter from which it was derived. For comfort reasons, the chassis was lengthened by 10 cm. The first version had the windscreen wiper pivoted from the roof and molding on the front bonnet. On the second, the windscreen wiper was in the conventional position while the front spare wheel compartment and rear engine cover had ample air intakes covered with wire gauze (picture right).

The **33 Stradale** was not a fortunate car; the company preferred the **Montreal** (but much later, given that production of the Bertone coupè did not begin until 1971). Eighteen **33 Stradale** cars were produced.

Chassis numbers not available, but they began with AR75033.101.

1750 GT VELOCE
(TYPE 105.44, ENGINE TYPE AR00548)
4 cylinders in line, 1779 cc, 118 hp, twin overhead camshafts. Wheelbase 2350 mm.

BERTONE COUPE'

The GT, which first appeared in 1963, was updated by the elimination of the imitation front air intake at the base of the bonnet and the introduction of double headlights. But it was the interior which received most attention. The dashboard was completely re-designed and given instruments with modern graphics, while the seats, which were extremely functional, had adjustable headrests which retracted into the seat backs. Powerful and elastic, the engine (132 hp SAE equal to 118 hp DIN) was used for the whole range including the Spider and, from 1968, also the saloon. **Chassis included between AR*1350001 and *1351040.**

1750 SPIDER VELOCE
(TYPE 105.57, ENGINE TYPE AR00548)
4 cylinders in line, 1779 cc, 118 hp, twin overhead camshafts. Wheelbase 2250 mm.

PININFARINA ROADSTER

There was little difference between this model and its predecessor, except for a new engine, three-spoke wood-rimmed steering wheel and, as with the previous version, the horn.
Chassis from AR*1410002 to *1410442 (including many cars produced in 1968).

The version destined for the U.S.A.

NO SIGNIFICANT MODIFICATIONS TO THE FOLLOWING MODELS:

Giulia T.I. (type 105.14). Just one car produced: chassis AR*468601.
Giulia T.I. (type 105.08). Chassis from AR*467532 to *468428.
Giulia Super (1965 version) **(type 105.26).** Chassis from AR*339977 to *349999
Giulia Sprint GT Veloce (type 105.36). Chassis from AR*246947 to *251106, from AR*251501 to *252902.
Giulia Sprint GT Veloce right hand drive **(type 105.37).** Chassis included between AR*298779 and *299870.
Giulia Sprint GTA (type 105.32 - 105.02/A). Chassis included between AR*613880 and *613980.
Gran Sport Quattroruote (type 101.23). Chassis included between AR*393046 and *393079
2600 (type 106.00). Chassis from AR*801581 to *801610.
2600 SZ (type 106.12). Chassis: AR*856004, *856079, *856086, from AR*856092 to *856105.

COMPETITION CARS NOT FOR PUBLIC SALE:
GIULIA TZ 2 (TYPE 105.11) - SPORTS SALOON FOR ROAD AND TRACK RACING
(except for AR10511*750117 which was especially built for the driver Aldo Bardelli)
GIULIA GTA SA (TYPE 105.32 - TYPE 105.02/A) (AUTODELTA) - FOR ROAD AND TRACK RACING
33 SPORT PROTOTYPES (AUTODELTA) - TWO-SEATER SPORTS FOR ROAD AND TRACK RACING

1968

1750
(TYPE 105.48, ENGINE TYPE AR00548)

4 cylinders in line, 1779 cc, 118 hp, twin overhead camshafts. Wheelbase 2570 mm.

ALFA ROMEO SALOON

The **1750** was an evolution of the Giulia, from which it retained the better parts. The new engine, which was already fitted to the GT Veloce and Spider Veloce, was a powerful four cylinder with a top speed of over 180 km/h. **Chassis from AR*1300104 to *1331381.**
1750 right hand drive (type 105.49). **Chassis from AR*1460003 to *1460451.**
1750 injection America (type 105.71). **Chassis from AR*1555001 to *1555143.**

SPIDER 1300 JUNIOR
(TYPE 105.91, ENGINE TYPE AR00530)

4 cylinders in line, 1290 cc, 89 hp, twin overhead camshafts. Wheelbase 2250 mm.

PININFARINA ROADSTER

As a result of the success of the GT 1300 Junior, the same engine had to give birth to a new model roadster given that, above all else, the production of the 1600 had ceased the previous year and the price list only included the more demanding **1750 Spider Veloce. Chassis from AR*1670001 to *1671920. Spider 1300 Junior** right hand drive (105.92). **Chassis from AR*1695001 to *1695101.**

GTA 1300 JUNIOR
(TYPE 105.59, ENGINE TYPE AR00559)

4 cylinders in line, 1290 cc, 96 hp, twin overhead camshafts. Wheelbase 2350 mm.

BERTONE COUPE'

Adopting the same body as the GTA but with the few corrections to make it look the same as the **GT 1300 Junior** (height of the rear wing, bulkhead separated from the boot, dashboard etc), an Alfa was born which was to dominate touring car racing right into the second half of the Seventies. Naturally, the engine had double ignition and there was magnesium alloy everywhere, just like its bigger 1600cc sister; the wheels of the production model were in steel as were those of the **Junior Zagato** and **1600 Junior Zagato**. A version prepared by Autodelta was also on the way but not in the price list: this had no bumper bars, was fitted with 14 inch Campagnolo *elektron* wheels, produced 160 hp, had a top speed of 210 km/h and a price of Lit 3,148,000. The Autodelta version, raced by both works and private drivers, continued through to the end of the Seventies (photo right).
Chassis included between AR*775001 and *776090.

GIULIA 1600 S
(TYPE 105.85, ENGINE TYPE AR00585)
4 cylinders in line, 1570 cc, 95 hp, twin overhead camshafts. Wheelbase 2510 mm.

ALFA ROMEO SALOON

This model substituted the **Giulia T.I.** which was no longer in production. The mechanics were updated in line with the other models in the range, except for the rear stabiliser bar, which it was decided would not be fitted as the vehicle was a touring car. The engine had a single twin-choke vertical carburettor.
Chassis included between AR*1700004 and *1700410.

NO SIGNIFICANT MODIFICATIONS TO THE FOLOWING MODELS:
Giulia 1300 (type 105.06). Chassis included between AR*649501 and *651700.
Giulia 1300 T.I. (type 105.39). Chassis from AR*656597 to *659999, from AR*1000501 to *1031243.
Giulia 1300 T.I. right hand drive **(type 105.40).** Chassis included between AR*763182 and *765032.
GT 1300 Junior (type 105.30). Chassis from AR*1215520 to *1230954.
GT 1300 Junior right hand drive **(type 105.31).** Chassis from AR*1290634 to *1291371.
Giulia T.I. (type 105.14). Chassis AR*468602 (only one car produced).
Giulia Super (type 105.26). Chassis from AR*869598 to *875769.
Giulia Sprint GT Veloce right hand drive **(type 105.37).** Chassis: AR*299852, *299854, *299864.
1750 GT Veloce (type 105.44). Chassis from AR*1351041 to *1359542, from AR*1361001 to *1362746.
1750 GT Veloce injection America (type 105.51). Chassis included between AR*1530002 and *1530152.
1750 GT Veloce right hand drive **(type 105.45).** Chassis from AR*1450001 to *1451061, from AR*1451501 to *1451061.
1750 Spider Veloce (type 105.57). Chassis included between AR*1410003 and *1411620 (including many cars produced in 1967); from AR*1411621 to *1411865.
1750 Spider Veloce injection America (type 105.62). Chassis from AR*1480001 to *1480216.
1750 Spider Veloce right hand drive **(type 105.58).** Chassis from AR*1470001 to *1470193.
2600 (type 106.00). Chassis from AR*801611 to *801637.
33 Stradale (type 105.33). Numbers not available.

NO CARS PRODUCED:
Giulia Sprint GTA (type 105.32 - type 105.02/A).

COMPETITION CARS NOT FOR PUBLIC SALE
GIULIA GTA SA (TYPE 105.32 - TYPE 105.02/A) (AUTODELTA) - FOR ROAD AND TRACK RACING
***33/2 DAYTONA* SPORTS PROTOTYPES** (AUTODELTA) - TWO-SEATER SPORT FOR ROAD AND TRACK RACING

1969

GIULIA 1300 T.I.
(TYPE 105.39, ENGINE TYPE AR00539)
4 cylinders in line, 1290 cc, 82 hp, twin overhead camshafts. Wheelbase 2510 mm.

ALFA ROMEO SALOON

Some modifications were carried out to the mechanics with the introduction of a hydraulic clutch and sprung pressure plate with diaphragm; the gearbox was also different with new synchronisers and a one-piece gear lever as reverse gear could be inserted without pushing. Braking stabilisers were added to the rear wheels and the engine mountings were changed, as were the elastic ball joints of the rear suspension. Externally, the bumper bars and their guards were made bigger.
Wheels and tyres in size 165-14 were optional.
Chassis from AR*1031244 to *1063444.

GT 1300 JUNIOR
(TYPE 105.30, ENGINE TYPE AR00530)
4 cylinders in line, 1290 cc, 89 hp, twin overhead camshafts. Wheelbase 2350 mm.

BERTONE COUPE'

As well as the mechanical modifications already described for the **Giulia 1300 T.I.**, a rear stabiliser bar was introduced. The most obvious interior modification was the new dashboard with more modern instruments very similar to those of the **1750 GT Veloce**. The internal ventilation system was completely revised.
Wheels and tyres in size 165-14 were optional.
Chassis from AR*1230955 to *1246008.

GIULIA SUPER

(TYPE 105.26, ENGINE TYPE AR00526/A)

4 cylinders in line, 1570 cc, 102 hp, twin overhead camshafts. Wheelbase 2510 mm.

ALFA ROMEO SALOON

The slight increase in engine power (4 hp) meant the car was given a new name. As well as all the modifications made to the **1300 T.I.** and the **GT 1300 Junior**, the Giulia Super was given a new dished steering wheel and, naturally, it was possible to have 165-14 tyres.
Chassis from AR*880001 to *897146.

1750 GT VELOCE

(TYPE 105.44, ENGINE TYPE AR00548)

4 cylinders in line, 1779 cc, 118 hp, twin overhead camshafts. Wheelbase 2350 mm.

BERTONE COUPE'

The updated version was unveiled at the Turin Motor Show with dual circuit brakes and pendant pedals. New carburettor filter with dynamic air intake. New seats with the fronts fitted with head rests, but which no longer retracted into the seat back. Heated rear window, iodine headlights, new bumper bars with rubber guards, new steering wheel and front sidelights.
Chassis from AR*1375004 to *1375700.

SPIDER 1300 JUNIOR
(TYPE 105.91, ENGINE TYPE AR00530)
4 cylinders in line, 1290 cc, 89 hp, twin overhead camshafts. Wheelbase 2250 mm.

Chassis from AR*1671921 to *1672700.

1750 SPIDER VELOCE
(TYPE 105.57, ENGINE TYPE AR00548)
4 cylinders in line, 1779 cc, 118 hp, twin overhead camshafts. Wheelbase 2250 mm.

Chassis from AR*1411866 to *1412788.

PININFARINA ROADSTER

The Spiders presented at the Turin Motor Show no longer had rounded tails, had a more inclined windscreen and pendant pedals. The 1300 had a simpler interior and some external differences (handles, headlights, etc).

The performance of both cars remained unchanged.
Spider 1300 Junior right hand drive (type 105.92). **Chassis from AR*1695201 to *1695279.**

1750 Spider Veloce injection Americana (type 105.62). **Chassis from AR*1480217 to *1481372.**
1750 Spider Veloce right hand drive (type 105.58). **Chassis from AR*1470301 to *1470601.**

1750

(TYPE 105.48, ENGINE TYPE AR00548)

4 cylinders in line, 1779 cc, 118 hp, twin overhead camshafts. Wheelbase 2570 mm.

ALFA ROMEO SALOON

The new 1750 saloon was also presented at the Turin Motor Show and the principal innovations were: dual circuit brakes; pendant pedals; new filter with dynamic air intake; iodine headlights; new tail lights; new steering wheel.
Chassis from AR*1740004 to *1742851.

NO SIGNIFICANT MODIFICATIONS TO THE FOLLOWING MODELS:

Giulia 1300 (type 105.06). Chassis from AR*1050001 to *1050136.
Giulia 1300 T.I. right hand drive **(type 105.40).** Chassis from AR*765033 to *765876.
GT 1300 Junior right hand drive **(type 105.31).** Chassis from AR*1291372 to *1291390.
GTA 1300 Junior (type 105.59). Chassis included between AR*775998 and *776147.
Spider 1300 Junior (type 105.91) (1st version). Chassis from AR*1671921 to *1672700.
Giulia 1600 S (type 105.85). Chassis included between AR*1700001 and *1701930.
Giulia 1600 S right hand drive **(type 105.87).** Chassis from AR*1790001 to *1790003.
Giulia Sprint GTA (type 105.32 - 105.02/A). Chassis from AR*848001 to *848012.
1750 (type 105.48) (1st version). Chassis from AR*1331382 to *1349498.
1750 GT Veloce (type 105.44) (1st version). Chassis from AR*1362747 to *1371827.
1750 GT Veloce injection America (type 105.51). Chassis included between AR*1530001 and *1530931.
1750 GT Veloce right hand drive **(type 105.45).** Chassis from AR*1451438 to *1453197.
1750 right hand drive **(type 105.49).** Chassis included between AR*1460920 and *1463346.
1750 injection America (type 105.71). Chassis from AR*1555144 to *1555825.
1750 Spider Veloce (type 105.57) (1st version). Chassis from AR*1411866 to *1412788.
2600 (type 106.00). Chassis from AR*801638 to *801640.
33 Stradale (type 105.33). Numbers not available.

COMPETITION CARS NOT FOR PUBLIC SALE
33/2 DAYTONA SPORT PROTOTYPES (AUTODELTA) - TWO-SEATER FOR ROAD AND TRACK RACING
33/3 SPORT PROTOTYPES (AUTODELTA) - TWO-SEATER FOR ROAD AND TRACK RACING

JUNIOR ZAGATO
(TYPE 105.93, ENGINE TYPE AR00530)

4 cylinders in line, 1290 cc, 89 hp, twin overhead camshafts. Wheelbase 2250 mm.

ZAGATO COUPE'

Chassis included between AR*1800004 and *1800624.

In 1969, deliveries began of the important new Junior Zagato, which was, unfortunately, subject to delays. Excellent work by the Milan body builder. The company designed a coupè which was a little too modern and even had a hatchback, an item of great success in later years. External bodywork was in steel, like the 2600 SZ, while the front grill which covered the lights was in plexiglass.

GIULIA 1300 SUPER
(TYPE 115.09, ENGINE TYPE AR00530)

4 cylinders in line, 1290 cc, 89 hp, twin overhead camshafts. Wheelbase 2510 mm.

ALFA ROMEO SALOON

Six years after its introduction, the performance of the 1300 saloon was increased with the adoption of the GT 1300 Junior's engine, obviously with two twin-choke carburettors. The braking system was modified with a dual circuit and the car was given pendant pedals. The interior was also updated: the seats of the Giulia Super 1600 were installed. Optional, 165-14 tyres.
Chassis from AR*2220008 to *2224815.

GT 1300 JUNIOR
(TYPE 105.30, ENGINE TYPE AR00530)

4 cylinders in line, 1290 cc, 89 hp, twin overhead camshafts. Wheelbase 2350 mm.

BERTONE COUPE'

The **GT 1300 Junior** exhibited at the Turin Motor Show was given the same front modifications as the **1750 GT Veloce**, except for the single optical group.
The bumper bars and tail lights were of a different shape. The mechanical modifications were the same as the **1300 Super** saloon (dual circuit braking system, pendant pedals, alternator). Optional, 165 SR14 tyres.
Chassis from AR*1260001 to *1262184.

SPIDER 1300 JUNIOR
(TYPE 105.91, ENGINE TYPE AR00530)
4 cylinders in line, 1290 cc, 89 hp, twin overhead camshafts. Wheelbase 2250 mm.

PININFARINA ROADSTER

The **Spider 1300 Junior** was updated in the same way as the **GT 1300 Junior** (dual circuit braking system, pendant pedals, alternator). Optional, 165-14 tyres.

Chassis from AR*1841003 to *1841128.

GIULIA SUPER
(TYPE 105.26, ENGINE TYPE AR00526/A)
4 cylinders in line, 1570 cc, 102 hp, twin overhead camshafts. Wheelbase 2510 mm.

ALFA ROMEO SALOON

Apart from modifications which extended throughout the range (dual circuit braking system, pendant pedals, alternator etc), the hand brake lever was mounted on the transmission tunnel and the choke on the steering column. The cigarette lighter was of new design. Optional, 165-14 tyres.
Chassis from AR*897147 to *899999.

NO SIGNIFICANT AESTHETIC MODIFICATIONS TO THE FOLLOWING MODELS (EXCEPT THE EXTENSION OF THE MECHANICAL UPDATING, THE DUAL CIRCUIT BRAKING SYSTEM AND PENDANT PEDALS):
Giulia 1300 (type 105.06). Chassis included between AR*1050137 and *1050431.
Giulia 1300 T.I. (type 105.39). Chassis from AR*1063445 to *1088763.
Giulia 1600 S (type 105.85). Chassis from AR*1701931 to *1702212.
1750 GT Veloce injection America (type 105.51). Chassis included between AR*1532001 and *1532269.
1750 Spider Veloce injection America (type 105.62). Chassis from AR*1485001 to *1485702.

NO SIGNIFICANT MODIFICATIONS TO THE FOLLOWING MODELS:
GT 1300 Junior (1969 version) **(type 105.30).** Chassis from AR*1246009 to *1257114.
GT 1300 Junior right hand drive **(type 105.31).** Chassis from AR*1292816 to *1293496.
Spider 1300 Junior (1969 version) **(type 105.91).** Chassis from AR*1840001 to *1840424; from AR*1841003 to *1841128.
GTA 1300 Junior (type 105.59). Chassis: AR*776001, *776011, *776012, *776016.
1750 (type 105.48). Chassis included between AR*1742852 and *1771455.
1750 right hand drive **(type 105.49).** Chassis from AR*1464001 to *1469680.
1750 injection America (type 105.71). Chassis from AR*1555826 to *1556091.
1750 GT Veloce (type 105.44). Chassis from AR*1375701 to *1387592.
1750 GT Veloce right hand drive **(type 105.45).** Chassis included between AR*1454001 and *1456101.
1750 GT Veloce injection America (type 105.51). Chassis included between AR*1530708 and *1531232.
1750 Spider Veloce (type 105.57). Chassis from AR*1820003 to *1820702.
1750 Spider Veloce injection America (type 105.62). Chassis from AR*1481373 to *1482220.

NO CARS PRODUCED:
1750 Spider Veloce right hand drive **(type 105.58).**

COMPETITION CARS NOT FOR PUBLIC SALE:
33/3 SPORT PROTOTYPES (AUTODELTA) - TWO-SEATER FOR ROAD AND TRACK RACING

1971

MONTREAL
(TYPE 105.64, ENGINE TYPE AR00564)

90° V8, 2593 cc, 200 hp, 4 overhead camshafts (2 per main bearing). Wheelbase 2350 mm.

BERTONE COUPE'

Introduced at the universal exposition in Montreal in 1967 during the celebration of the 100th anniversary of the Canadian Federation and equipped with a Giulia engine, the car was designed by Carrozzeria Bertone. It did not go into production until 1971, although various prototypes and pre-series examples were made; the company had even established the colour range as far back as 1968. A new presentation of the car took place at the Geneva Motor Show in 1970. During its long gestation period, which unfortunately noticeably obscured its optimum qualities, the car was definitively given the prestigious engine derived from that of the **33**, its performance suitably reduced. **Chassis included between AR*1425101 and *1426123.**

2000
(TYPE 105.12, ENGINE TYPE AR00512)

4 cylinders in line, 1962 cc, 132 hp, twin overhead camshafts. Wheelbase 2570 mm.

ALFA ROMEO SALOON

Few aesthetic modifications compared to the **1750** saloon: the shield was a little wider, the sidelights somewhat bigger and the wheelnuts were visible. The tail remained unchanged but the optical group was of different design and size.

The car could be bought with anti-blocking differential, heated rear window, front seat headrests and metallic paint.

The car's press presentation took place at Gardone in June.

It is probable that the increase in engine power to two litres came from the optimum reliability of the **GT Am**, the **1750 GT Veloce** racing car modified by Autodelta. The cubic capacity of its engine was increased by working on the bore. **Chassis from AR*2300001 to *2316450.**

The **2000** with the right hand drive (105.15).

Chassis from AR*2400001 to *2400600.

2000 GT VELOCE
(TYPE 105.21, ENGINE TYPE AR00512)

4 cylinders in line, 1962 cc, 132 hp, twin overhead camshafts. Wheelbase 2350 mm.

BERTONE COUPE'

The same mechanics as the **2000** saloon but with a longer axle ratio and auto-blocking differential as original equipment to avoid problems caused by the engine's high performance accompanied by optimum torque. The component became indispensable; taking a tight corner at high speed, the inside rear wheel lifted without the car losing traction. Compared to the **1750 GT Veloce**, the dashboard instruments were modified and the seats were of new design. **Chassis from AR*2420001 to *2427650. 2000 GT Veloce** right hand drive (**type 105.22**). **Chassis from AR*2410001 to *2410250.**

2000 SPIDER VELOCE
(TYPE 105.24, ENGINE TYPE AR00512)

4 cylinders in line, 1962 cc, 132 hp, twin overhead camshafts. Wheelbase 2250 mm.

PININFARINA ROADSTER

The **2000 GT Veloce** mechanical modifications were also made to this car, the only difference being the capacity of the petrol tank: 51 litres instead of 53. No aesthetic modifications, with the exception of the rear script and the wheels without hub caps, which were still present on the previous versions. **Chassis from AR*2460001 to *2460850. 2000 Spider Veloce** right hand drive (**type 105.27**). **Chassis from AR*2470001 to *2470125.**

NO SIGNIFICANT MODIFICATIONS TO THE FOLLOWING MODELS:
Giulia 1300 (type 105.06). Chassis included between AR*1050384 and *1050433.
Giulia 1300 T.I. (type 105.39). Chassis from AR*1088764 to *1089439.
Giulia 1300 Super (type 115.09). Chassis from AR*2224816 to *2263009.
Giulia 1300 Super right hand drive (**type 115.10**). Chassis from AR*2294002 to *2295366.
GT 1300 Junior (type 105.30). Chassis from AR*1262185 to *1276549.
GT 1300 Junior right hand drive (**type 105.31**). Chassis from AR*1295001 to *1295820.
Junior Zagato (type 105.93). Chassis included between AR*1800435 and *1800970.
Spider 1300 Junior (type 105.91). Chassis from AR*1841129 to *1841874.
GTA 1300 Junior (type 105.59). Chassis: AR*776027, *776029, *776047, *776061, *776066, *776070, *776074, *776076, *776079, *776088, *776089, *776091, *776095, *776106, *776116, *776123, *776124, *776133, *776150, *776160, *776166.
Giulia Super (type 105.26). Chassis from AR*1875004 to *1891387.
1750 (type 105.48). Chassis from AR*1780001 to *1780253.
1750 GT Veloce (type 105.44). Chassis from AR*1387593 to *1391721.
1750 GT Veloce right hand drive (**type 105.45**). Chassis included between AR*1456167 and *1456902.
1750 GT Veloce injection America (type 105.51). Chassis included between AR*1532004 and *1533244.
1750 Spider Veloce (type 105.57). Chassis from AR*1820703 to *1820263.
1750 Spider Veloce right hand drive (**type 105.58**). Chassis from AR*1835001 to *1835141 (oil filter on the right).
1750 Spider Veloce injection America (type 105.62). Chassis included between AR*1485703 and *1486880.

COMPETITION CARS NOT FOR PUBLIC SALE
33/3 SPORT PROTOTYPES (AUTODELTA) - TWO-SEATER SPORT FOR RACING ON ROAD AND TRACK
33 TT 3 (AUTODELTA) - TWO-SEATER SPORT FOR RACING ON ROAD AND TRACK

ALFETTA
(TYPE 116.08, ENGINE AR01608)
4 cylinders in line, 1779 cc, 122 hp, twin overhead camshafts. Wheelbase 2510 mm.

SALOON

After a rather long gestation period due to involvement in the **Alfasud** project (the car was due to appear the previous year) the **Alfetta** was introduced in May. Even though the engine was well-known, tried and tested by the **1750**, the torsion bar front suspension and completely re-designed body rendered the car new and modern. But the real masterpiece was its De Dion rear axle with gearbox, stubbornly championed by its designer Giuseppe Busso, who had already tested the system with success on a number of racing cars. The gearbox incorporated in the differential group created a perfect equilibrium of weight to the advantage of driving safety and stability when cornering and braking.
Chassis from AR*2001001 to *2021350.
Alfetta right hand drive (**type 116.09**). **Chassis from AR*2160002 to *2160331.**

GIULIA SUPER 1.3
(TYPE 115.09, ENGINE TYPE AR00530)
4 cylinders in line, 1290 cc, 89 hp, twin overhead camshafts. Wheelbase 2510 mm.

ALFA ROMEO SALOON

The **Giulia 1300 Super** was, by this time, called the **Giulia Super 1.3** and was improved in line with the **Giulia Super**. The production of the latter ceased but the 1600 engine which, obviously, equipped the **Giulia Super 1.6**, (type 105.26, engine AR00526) for a long time, could be fitted to the 1.3.
The front was re-newed by the adoption of four headlights, there was a new optical group and new script to the rear; the wheels had no hub caps.
The steering wheel had three spokes; the seats were modified and a new retractable rear armrest was added; new dashboard with electric clock; opening of the air vents with a rotating handle.
Chassis from AR*2272001 to *2289600.
Giulia Super 1.3 right hand drive (type 115.10). **Chassis included between AR*2295367 and *2297279.**

GT 1300 JUNIOR
(TYPE 105.30, ENGINE TYPE AR00530)

4 cylinders in line, 1290 cc, 89 hp, twin overhead camshafts. Wheelbase 2350 mm.

BERTONE COUPE'

Chassis from AR*1276550 to *1279410 and from AR*1281001 to *1284564.

SPIDER 1300 JUNIOR
(TYPE 105.91, ENGINE TYPE AR00530)

4 cylinders in line, 1290 cc, 89 hp, twin overhead camshafts. Wheelbase 2250 mm.

PININFARINA ROADSTER

From May the wheels, fitted with 165 SR 14 tyres, no longer wore hub caps and their nuts were in view, as with the saloon range. No other aesthetic or technical variations for either model. **Chassis from AR*1841875 to *1842445.**

GT 1600 JUNIOR
(TYPE 115.03, ENGINE TYPE AR00536)

4 cylinders in line, 1570 cc, 109 hp, twin overhead camshafts. Wheelbase 2350 mm.

BERTONE COUPE'

After a long break, production resumed in May of the GT with the 1600 engine. The body was of the **GT 1300 Junior** but, while conserving the previous serial number, the engine was re-designed: the most obvious feature was the cartridge oil filter, fixed to the timing case instead of an oil bath filter as with previous versions.
Tyres 165 x 14 and the elimination of the hub caps.

Chassis from AR*2195001 to *2198850.
GT 1600 Junior right hand drive (type 115.05). **Chassis from AR*2205001 to *2205900**

SPIDER 1600 JUNIOR
(TYPE 115.07, ENGINE TYPE AR00536)

4 cylinders in line, 1570 cc, 109 hp, twin overhead camshafts. Wheelbase 2250 mm.

PININFARINA ROADSTER

Spider 1600 production resumed: the car was the same as the 1300 except for its engine, equipped with a cartridge filter identical to that of the **GT 1600 Junior**.
Tyres 165 SR 14 with wheel nuts visible.
Chassis from AR*2208001 to *2208950.

Giulia Super 1.3, GT and Spider.

ALFASUD

(TYPE 901A, ENGINE TYPE AS30100)

4 cylinders horizontally opposed, 1186 cc, 63 hp, 1
overhead camshaft per main bearing. Wheelbase 2455 mm.

ALFA ROMEO SALOON

Unveiled at the Turin Motor Show
in November, 1971, and then
officially at Pomigliano d'Arco,
delivery of the revolutionary front-
wheel drive small car with a boxer
engine began in June, 1972.
This was a completely new project
for Alfa Romeo and the result of
considerable work by the late
engineer Rudolf Hruska, who died
in 1995, and engineer Domenico
Chirico.
**Chassis from AS*5000001*901A
to *5022350*901A.**

1600 JUNIOR ZAGATO

(TYPE 115.24, ENGINE TYPE AROO536*S)

4 cylinders in line, 1570 cc, 109 hp, twin overhead camshafts. Wheelbase 2250 mm.

ZAGATO COUPE'

The platform of the **Spider 1600
Junior** and the body of the **Junior
Zagato**: it was from this marriage
that the new Zagato coupè was
born.
The coupè's appearance was
slightly different to the 1300: front
bumpers of different design; a
new type of rear optical group
incorporating a reversing light; the
end of the exhaust pipe turned
down towards the ground; wood-
rimmed steering wheel with horn
pressure pads on all three spokes.
**Chassis from AR*3060000 to
*3060099.**

NO SIGNIFICANT MODIFICATIONS TO THE FOLLOWING MODELS:
Giulia 1300 T.I. (type 105.39). Chassis from AR*1089440 to *1089493.
Giulia 1300 Super (1ˢᵗ version) **(type 115.09).** Chassis from AR*2263010 to *2269104.
Junior Zagato (type 105.93). Chassis included between AR*1800519 and *1801117.
GTA 1300 Junior (type 105.59). Chassis: AR*776038, *776053, *776067, *776077, *776083, *776085, *776138, *776152, *776153, *776156, *776157, *776163, *776164, *776165.
Giulia Super (type 105.26). Chassis from AR*1891388 to *1896477.
Giulia Super 1.6 (type 105.26). Chassis from AR*1980001 to *1986620.
Giulia Super 1.6 right hand drive **(type 105.28).** Chassis AR*0786001 to *0786665.
1750 injection America (type 105.49). Only one car produced: chassis AR*1557001
1750 GT Veloce (type 105.44). Only one car built after production ceased in September, 1971: chassis AR*1391722.
1750 GT Veloce injection America (type 105.51). Chassis: AR*1532052, *1533142, *1533169, *1533201, *1533217; from AR*1533221 to *1533223, *1533229, *1533234.
2000 (type 105.12). Chassis from AR*2316451 to *2345650.
2000 right hand drive **(type 105.15).** Chassis from AR*2400601 to *2403941.
2000 injection America (type 115.00). Chassis from AR*3000001 to *3000800.
2000 GT Veloce (type 105.21). Chassis from AR*2420001 to *2427650.
2000 GT Veloce right hand drive **(type 105.22).** Chassis from AR*2410251 to *2412050.
2000 GT Veloce injection America (type 115.01). Chassis from AR*3020001 to *3020951; from AR*3021501 to *3021717.
2000 Spider Veloce (type 105.24). Chassis from AR*2460851 to *2462300.
2000 Spider Veloce right hand drive **(type 105.27).** Chassis from AR*2470126 to *2470450.
2000 Spider Veloce injection America (type 115.02). Chassis from AR*3040001 to *3040818; from AR*3041001 to *3041200
Montreal (type 105.64). Chassis included between AR*1425108 and *1428201.

COMPETITION CAR NOT FOR PUBLIC SALE
33 TT 3 (AUTODELTA) - TWO-SEATER FOR RACING ON ROAD AND TRACK

1973

ALFASUD
(TYPE 901A, ENGINE TYPE AS30100)
4 cylinders horizontally opposed, 1186 cc, 63 hp,
1 overhead camshaft per main bearing. Wheelbase 2455 mm.

ALFA ROMEO SALOON

The brake servo was introduced in June. On request, heated rear window; from November the horn was replaced and a cigarette lighter, rev counter and headrests could be fitted as options.
Chassis from AS*5022351*901A to *5099900*901A.

ALFASUD ti
(TYPE 901C, ENGINE TYPE AS30104)
4 cylinders horizontally opposed, 1186 cc, 68 hp,
1 overhead camshaft per main bearing. Wheelbase 2455 mm.

ALFA ROMEO SALOON

The main feature was that the car had only two doors. A rear spoiler was also added, plus a suggestion of aerodynamics below the front bumper. The interior was almost completely re-designed and the adjustable steering wheel had three spokes. The gearbox was five speed, the carburettor was twin-choke and a series of other improvements silenced the critics of the previous model.
The car was unveiled in November.
Chassis from AS*5320011*901C to *5321450*901C.

1973

The three Giulias.

NO SIGNIFICANT MODIFICATIONS TO THE FOLLOWING MODELS:

Alfasud (type 901A). Chassis from AS*5022351*901A to *5099900*901A.

Giulia Super 1.3 (type 115.09). Chassis from AR*2289601 to *2292999, from AR*3320001 to *3334850.

Giulia Super 1.3 right hand drive **(type 115.10).** Chassis from AR*2297280 to *2297900.

Giulia Super 1.6 (type 105.26). Chassis from AR*1986621 to *1995700.

GT 1300 Junior (type 105.30). Chassis from AR*1284565 to *1289999, from AR*3350001 to *3350350.

GTA 1300 Junior (type 105.59). Chassis: AR*776054, *776071, *776093, ***776100, *776105,** *776107, *776109, *776111, *776112, *776114, *776120, *776127, *776128, *776130, *776137, *776140, *776142, *776146, *776149, *776155, *776162, *776167.

Spider 1300 Junior (type 105.91). Chassis from AR*1842446 to *1843259.

GT 1600 Junior (type 115.03). Chassis from AR*2198851 to *2202250.

GT 1600 Junior right hand drive **(type 115.05).** Chassis from AR*2205901 to *2206700.

Spider 1600 Junior (type 115.07). Chassis from AR*2208951 to *2209900.

1600 Junior Zagato (type 115.24). Chassis from AR*3060100 to *3060402.

Alfetta (type 116.08). Chassis from AR*2021351 to *2061900.

Alfetta right hand drive **(type 116.09).** Chassis from AR*000101 to *0004451 (including all cars produced in 1974 and some in 1975).

1750 GT Veloce injection America (type 105.51). Only one car produced: chassis AR*1532002.

2000 (type 105.12). Chassis from AR*2345651 to *2366500.

2000 right hand drive **(type 105.15).** Chassis from AR*2403942 to *2404831, from AR*2405512 to *2406500.

2000 injection America (type 115.00). Chassis from AR*3001251 to *3001900.

2000 GT Veloce (type 105.21). Chassis from AR*2433791 to *2444050.

2000 GT Veloce right hand drive **(type 105.22).** Chassis from AR*2412051 to *2413734.

2000 GT Veloce injection America (type 115.01). Chassis from AR*3021718 to *3022800.

2000 Spider Veloce (type 105.24). Chassis from AR*2462301 to *2463385, from AR*3060100 to *3060402.

2000 Spider Veloce right hand drive **(type 105.27).** Chassis from AR*2470451 to *2470700.

2000 Spider Veloce injection America (type 115.02). Chassis from AR*3041201 to *3042309, from AR*3042501 to *3042750.

Montreal (type 105.64). Chassis included between AR*1425178 and *1428858.

Montreal right hand drive **(type 105.65).** Chassis included between AR*1440101 and *1440326 (including those produced in 1974 and 1975).

NO CARS PRODUCED:
Junior Zagato (type 105.93).

COMPETITION CAR NOT FOR PUBLIC SALE
33/3 TT 12 (AUTODELTA) - TWO-SEATER FOR ROAD AND TRACK RACING

1974

ALFETTA GT
(TYPE 116.10, ENGINE TYPE AR01608*S)

4 cylinders in line, 1779 cc, 122 hp, twin overhead camshafts. Wheelbase 2400 mm.

ALFA ROMEO COUPE'

Apart from the reduction in wheelbase, the platform was the same as the saloon's but the refinement of the mechanics and weight distribution made this a magnificent grand tourer. **Chassis from AR11610*0001011 to *0007800.**

NUOVA SUPER 1.3
(TYPE 115.09S, ENGINE TYPE AR00530*S)

4 cylinders in line, 1290 cc, 89 hp, twin overhead camshafts. Wheelbase 2510 mm.

Chassis from AR11509*0001001 to *0018100.

NUOVA SUPER 1.6
(TYPE 105.26S, ENGINE TYPE AR00526A*S)

4 cylinders in line, 1570 cc, 102 hp, twin overhead camshafts. Wheelbase 2510 mm.

Chassis from AR10526*0001001 to *0008250 (numbering system in common with the Nuova Super 1.3).

ALFA ROMEO SALOON

Twelve years after its introduction, the Giulia received a number of radical modifications which smoothed out the bonnet and boot lid. The re-styling operation took away part of the classic saloon's personality, but succeeded in re-launching it in the market. The four headlights were of the same diameter, the bumpers newly designed with rubber guards, the radiator grill was painted black. Wood-rimmed steering wheel with three spokes, new-design dashboard and re-newed seating. The car was presented at Fonteblanda near Grossetto in June.

GT 1300 JUNIOR
(TYPE 105.30S, ENGINE TYPE AR00530*S)

4 cylinders in line, 1290 cc, 89 hp, twin overhead camshafts. Wheelbase 2350 mm.

Chassis from AR10530*0001001 to *0003650.

GT 1600 JUNIOR
(TYPE 115.34, ENGINE TYPE AR00526A*S)

4 cylinders in line, 1570 cc, 109 hp, twin overhead camshafts. Wheelbase 2350 mm.

Chassis from AR11534*0001051 to *0001372.

BERTONE COUPE'

The last update of the **GT 1300 Junior**, which first appeared in 1966, was of the engines and the unification of the body with that of the **2000 GT Veloce.**
The interior (dashboard, seats, other details) also reflected those of the bigger sister.
The car was presented in June, together with the Nuova Super.

SPIDER 1300 JUNIOR
(TYPE 105.91S, ENGINE TYPE AR00530*S)

4 cylinders in line, 1290 cc, 89 hp, twin overhead camshafts. Wheelbase 2250 mm.

PININFARINA ROADSTER

In June, the Spider 1300 Junior assumed a new type designation. Performance was unchanged, while the car's equipment in general was given a number of modifications, of which the most important was two occasional seats behind the fronts. **Chassis from AR10591*0001001 to *0001457.**

ALFASUD
(TYPE 901D1, ENGINE TYPE AS30102)

4 cylinders horizontally opposed, 1186 cc, 63 hp, 1 overhead camshaft per main bearing. Wheelbase 2455 mm.

ALFA ROMEO SALOON

The windscreen wiper arms were painted matt black and the carburettor was modified to improve petrol circulation.
Elasticised drive was adopted to reduce steering wheel vibration. **Chassis from AS*5000001*901D to *5000500*901D.**

ALFASUD L
ALFASUD N
(TYPE 901D, ENGINE TYPE AS30102)
4 cylinders horizontally opposed, 1186 cc, 63 hp, 1 overhead camshaft per main bearing. Wheelbase 2455 mm.

ALFA ROMEO SALOON

Production of the luxury version began, although the car would not go on sale until January, 1975. These modifications: horizontal chrome strips for the radiator grill, rubber guards for the bumper bars, shiny profile at the base of the side panels, new script on the tail. Interior: bigger grip steering wheel, new dashboard padded in the central area, lockable glove box, ashtrays also in the rear door armrests, electric windscreen washers and new-design illuminated heater controls, rev counter on request. The production of the base version, by then called the N,

continued in parallel with its more economical finish.
Chassis from AS*5000001*901D to *5000500*901D (in common with the type 901D1).**

ALFETTA 1.6
(TYPE 116.00, ENGINE TYPE AR01600)
4 cylinders in line, 1570 cc, 108 hp, twin overhead camshafts. Wheelbase 2510 mm.

ALFA ROMEO SALOON

The less expensive version of the **Alfetta** had a more spartan finish: only two headlights although of large diameter, black radiator grill with only one shiny horizontal bar and bumper bars without rubber guards; the windscreen wiper blades were in matt black and the rear ventilation grills in black plastic. The steering wheel rim was covered in imitation leather instead of wood; there were no pockets in the backs of the front seats and the central console was not decorated with imitation wood. Compared to the 1.8, the advantages of this model were all in the performance/consumption ratio. The car had a lower maximum speed of only 5 km but consumption was much reduced. The mechanics were identical to those of the 1.8, with the exception of the engine which was from the **Nuova Super 1600** with 9 horse power more.

Deliveries began in January, 1975.
Chassis from AR11600*0001001 to *0005500.

NO SIGNIFICANT MODIFICATIONS TO THE FOLLOWING MODELS:

Alfasud (type 901A). Chassis from AS*5099901*901A to *5168400*901A.

Alfasud ti (type 901C). Chassis from AS*5321451*901C to *5351442* 901C.

Giulia Super 1.3 (type 115.09). Chassis from AR*3334851 to *3340250.

Giulia Super 1.3 right hand drive **(type 115.10).** Chassis from AR*2297901 to *2299450.

GT 1300 Junior (type 105.30). Chassis from AR*3350351 to *3351550.

GTA 1300 Junior (type 105.59). Chassis: AR*776122, *776125, *776129, *776134, *776151, *776158, *776159.

Junior Zagato (type 105.93). Chassis: AR*1800001, *1800003.

Giulia Super 1.6 (type 105.26). Chassis from AR*1995701 to *1998088.

Giulia Super 1.6 right hand drive **(type 105.28).** Chassis from AR*0787826 to *0788006.

GT 1600 Junior (type 115.03). Chassis from AR*2202251 to *2203344.

GT 1600 Junior right hand drive **(type 115.05).** Chassis from AR*2206701 to *2207010.

Spider 1600 Junior (type 115.07). Chassis from AR*2209901 to *2210100, from AR*0001001 to *0001070.

Spider 1600 Junior (type 115.35). Chassis from AR*0001001 to *0001106.

Alfetta (type 116.08). Chassis from AR*2061901 to *2105454.

Alfetta right hand drive **(type 116.09).** Chassis from AR*000101 to *0004451 (including all cars produced in 1973 and some in 1975).

2000 (type 105.12). Chassis AR*2366501 to *2372100.

2000 right hand drive **(type 105.15).** Chassis from AR*2406501 to *2406637.

2000 GT Veloce (type 105.21). Chassis from AR*2444051 to *2445676.

2000 GT Veloce right hand drive **(type 105.22).** Chassis from AR*2413735 to *2414649 (including cars produced in 1975)

2000 GT Veloce injection America (type 115.01). Chassis from AR*3023001 to *3023900.

2000 Spider Veloce (type 105.24). Chassis from AR*2463386 to *2464135.

2000 Spider Veloce right hand drive **(type 105.27).** Chassis from AR*2470701 to *247010

2000 Spider Veloce injection America (type 115.02). Chassis from AR*3042751 to *30462509.

Montreal (type 105.64). Chassis included between AR*1428219 and *1428719.

Montreal right hand drive **(type 105.65).** Chassis included between AR*1440101 and *1440326 (including cars made in 1973 and 1975).

COMPETITION CAR NOT FOR PUBLIC SALE
33/3 TT 12 (AUTODELTA) - TWO-SEATER SPORT FOR ROAD AND TRACK RACING

ALFASUD GIARDINETTA

(TYPE 904A, ENGINE TYPE AS30102)

4 cylinders horizontally opposed, 1186 cc, 63 hp, 1 camshaft
per main bearing. Wheelbase 2455 mm.

STATION WAGON

This vehicle had the technical characteristics of the normal model, but with the finish of the luxury version plus heated rear window. The design of the station wagon was very successful; the hatchback was functional, the floor low and without obstacles. Unfortunately, the car's sales success did not come up to expectations.
Chassis from AS*5000001*904A to *5005450*904A.

ALFETTA 1.8

(TYPE 116.42, ENGINE TYPE AR01608*X)

4 cylinders in line, 1779 cc, 118 hp, twin overhead camshafts. Wheelbase 2510 mm.

SALOON

In May the **Alfetta**, now designated the 1.8 to distinguish it from the rest of the range, was given a series of updates which were: larger shield on the radiator grill, door mirrors, adjustable headrests, electric windscreen washer and central oddments box like that of the GT. Carburation was improved for better consumption, but with a power loss of 4 hp.
Chassis from AR*2107001 to *2121900.
Alfetta right hand drive (**type 116.09**).
Chassis from AR*0001001 to *0004451 (including cars produced in 1973 and 1974), from AR*0005001 to *0006121.

(*) **Note:**
With the exception of the Spider and the last of the **2000 GT Veloce** model, from 1975 the cars were designed and prepared by the Centro Stile Alfa Romeo (Alfa Romeo Styling Centre) and built by the company itself.

ALFETTA GT 1.8
(TYPE 116.54, ENGINE TYPE AR01608*X)

4 cylinders in line, 1779 cc, 118 hp, twin overhead camshafts. Wheelbase 2400 mm.

COUPE'

The proliferation of engines of different cubic capacities for the **Alfetta GT** obliged the company to introduce a new denomination for this model.
Power was reduced by 4 hp.
Chassis from AR*0001001 to *0001800.
Alfetta GT right hand drive (type 116.11). **Chassis from AR11654*0001001 to *0002900,** from AR11654*3370001 to *3370820.

2000
(TYPE 115.36, ENGINE TYPE AR00515)

4 cylinders in line, 1962 cc, 129 hp, twin overhead camshafts. Wheelbase 2570 mm.

SALOON

Electronic ignition and the transistorised induction capacity took three horse power from this car's potent engine, but that was compensated for by easier cold starting and better operation at every revolution.
Rear headrests were added to the interior, while the fronts became reclinable; electric windscreen washers; new steering wheel boss and new gear lever knob.
Chassis from AR*2375001 to *2378450.
2000 right hand drive (type 105.15). **Chassis from AR*2406638 to *2408105.**

2000 SPIDER VELOCE
(TYPE 115.38, ENGINE TYPE AR00515)

4 cylinders in line, 1962 cc, 132 hp, twin overhead camshafts. Wheelbase 2250 mm.

PININFARINA ROADSTER

As had previously happened with the **Spider 1300 Junior**, the **2000 Spider Veloce** was also given a 2+2 body. No change in performance.
Chassis from AR11538*2465001 to *2465780.

The America version of the
2000 Spider Veloce.

NO SIGNIFICANT MODIFICATIONS TO THE FOLLOWING MODELS:

Alfasud (type 901A). Chassis from AS*5168401*901A to *5176850*901A.

Alfasud L, Alfasud N (type 901D). Chassis from AS*5000501*901D to *5078500*901D.

Alfasud ti (type 901C). Chassis from AS*5351443*901C to *5420287* 901C.

Nuova Super 1.3 (type 115.09S). Chassis from AR11509*0018101 to *0039250.

GT 1300 Junior (type 105.30S). Chassis from AR10530*0003651 to *0005200.

GTA 1300 Junior (type 105.59). Chassis: AR*776006, *776050, *776063, *776080, *776092, *776099, *776103, *776115, *776119, *776121, *776126, *776131, *776139, *776144, *776148.

Spider 1300 Junior (type 105.91S). Chassis from AR10591*0001458 to *0002000.

Nuova Super 1.6 (type 105.26S). Chassis from AR10526*0008251 to 016450.

Nuova Super 1.6 right hand drive **(type 105.28).** Chassis from AR10528*0001001 to *0001161.

GT 1600 Junior (type 115.03). Chassis from AR*0002051 to *0002600.

GT 1600 Junior (type 115.34). Chassis from AR11534*0001373 to *0002020.

GT 1600 Junior right hand drive **(type 115.05).** Chassis from AR*2207011 to *2207210, from AR*0001001 to *0002057.

Spider 1600 Junior (type 115.35). Chassis from AR11535*0001107 to *0001450.

Alfetta 1.6 (type 116.00). Chassis from AR11600*0005501 to *0020900.

Alfetta GT (type 116.10). Chassis from AR11610*0007801 to *0015584.

Alfetta GT right hand drive **(type 116.11).** Chassis from AR11611*0001001 to *0002900, from AR11611*3370001 to *3370820.

2000 (type 105.12). Chassis from AR*2372101 to *2372429.

2000 GT Veloce (type 105.21). Chassis from AR*2445677 to *2446580.

2000 GT Veloce right hand drive **(type 105.22).** Chassis from AR*2413735 to *2414649 (including all cars produced in 1974).

2000 GT Veloce injection America (type 115.01). Chassis from AR*3025901 to *3027089.

2000 Spider Veloce right hand drive **(type 105.27).** Chassis from AR*2471011 to *2471060, from AR*2472001 to *2472270.

2000 Spider Veloce injection America (type 115.02). Chassis from AR*3046251 to *3046771, from AR*3047001 to *3048900.

Montreal (type 105.64). Chassis: AR*1427789, *1427794, *1428001, *1428050, *1428061, *1428186, *1428191, *1427492, *1428054, *1428124.

Montreal right hand drive **(type 105.65).** Chassis included between *1440101 and *1440326 (including cars produced in 1973 and 1974).

COMPETITION CARS NOT FOR PUBLIC SALE

MARTINI-BRABHAM-ALFA ROMEO (BRABHAM-AUTODELTA) - SINGLE-SEATER FORMULA ONE CAR
33 TT 12 (AUTODELTA) - TWO-SEATER SPORT FOR ROAD AND TRACK RACING
ALFETTA GT (AUTODELTA)- FOR ROAD AND TRACK RACING

ALFETTA GT 1.6
(TYPE 116.04, ENGINE TYPE AR01600)
4 cylinders in line, 1570 cc, 108 hp, twin overhead camshafts. Wheelbase 2400 mm.

COUPE'

The 1600cc engine, which retained the bore and stroke of the Giulia, was installed in the 1.8 bodyshell. Above the rear number plate was the large Alfa Romeo script and the dashboard differed from that of the 2000 by the incorporation of a long strip of wood.
Chassis from AR11604*0001001 to *0004600.
Alfetta GT 1.6 right hand drive (type 116.02). **Chassis from AR11602*0001771 to *0002000, from AR11602*0002101 to *0002310.**

Alloy wheels were supplied as optional equipment.

ALFETTA GTV 2000
(TYPE 116.36. ENGINE TYPE AR01623)
4 cylinders in line, 1962 cc, 122 hp, twin overhead camshafts. Wheelbase 2400 mm.

COUPE'

Compared to the 1.8 bodyshell, the differences were minimal: rubber guards for the bumper bars which were absent on the 1.6, triangular rear air outlet with prominent GTV script. As with the 1.6, the Alfa Romeo script was placed above the rear number plate. The steel wheels were of different design, no longer with round holes as they were from the introduction of the Giulia, and alloy wheels were optional.
Chassis from AR11636*0001001 to *0010950.
Alfetta GTV 2000 right hand drive (type 116.37).
Chassis from AR11637*0001001 to *0001900.

ALFASUD SPRINT
(TYPE 902A, ENGINE TYPE AS30184)

4 cylinders horizontally opposed, 1286 cc, 87 hp SAE, 1 overhead camshaft per main bearing. Wheelbase 2455 mm.

COUPE'

Sprint is a term which defined an epoch; it was brought back for the new **Alfasud** coupè. The development of the line was entrusted to Giugiaro and the saloon mechanicals were adopted. **Chassis from AS*5000001*902A to *5006350*902A.**

ALFASUD 5 MARCE
(TYPE 901D, ENGINE TYPE AS30102)

4 cylinders horizontally opposed, 1186 cc, 63 hp, 1 overhead camshaft per main bearing. Wheelbase 2455 mm.

SALOON

From July, the **Alfasud** saloon became available with a five-speed gearbox. No other changes. **Chassis from AS*5078501*901D to *5087103*901D, from AS*5100001*901D to *5141747*901D, from AS*5150001*901D to *5158899*901D.**

ALFASUD GIARDINETTA
(TYPE 904A1, ENGINE TYPE AS30102)

4 cylinders horizontally opposed, 1186 cc, 63 hp, 1 overhead camshaft per main bearing. Wheelbase 2455 mm.

STATION WAGON

The most important change was the adoption of the five-speed gearbox. **Chassis from AS*5005451*904A to *7007000*904A.**

GIULIA DIESEL

(TYPE 115.40, ENGINE TYPE 108U)
4 cylinders in line, 1760 cc, 52 hp, 1 lateral camshaft in crankcase.
Wheelbase 2510.

SALOON

The last Giulia was the diesel, which was introduced when the model had most certainly been overtaken. The engine was by Perkins which, for some years, had been supplying motors for the **F 12** people carrier.
The car's appearance remained the same as the petrol-engined models, except for the script on the tail. The engine compartment was amply insulated with about five kilos of sound-deadening material. This was a mild attempt at evaluating the response of the market to a solution adopted by a company which, by tradition, did not favour slow and economical Diesel engines.
Chassis from AR11540*0001011 to *0007592.

NO SIGNIFICANT MODIFICATIONS TO THE FOLLOWING MODELS:
Alfasud ti (type 901C). Chassis from AS*5420288*901C to *5454448*901C.
Alfasud Giardinetta (type 904A). Chassis from AS*5005451*904A to *7007000*904A (in common with type 904A1).
Nuova Super 1.3 (type 115.09S). Chassis from AR11509*0039251 to *0053050.
Spider 1300 Junior (type 105.91S). Chassis from AR10591*0002001 to *0002461.
Nuova Super 1.6 (type 105.26S). Chassis from AR10526*0016451 to *0020850.
Nuova Super 1.6 right hand drive **(type 105.28).** Chassis from AR10528*3083341 to *3083420.
Spider 1600 Junior (type 115.35). Chassis from AR11535*0001451 to *0001800.
Alfetta 1.6 (type 116.00). Chassis from AR11600*0020901 to *0044604
Alfetta 1.8 (type 116.42). Chassis from AR*2121901 to *2152865.
Alfetta right hand drive **(type 116.09).** Chassis from AR*0006122 to *0006681.
Alfetta GT right hand drive **(type 116.11).** Chassis from AR*0002901 to *0003258.
Alfetta GT 1.8 (type 116.54). Chassis from AR11654*0001801 to *0005308.
Alfetta GT 1.8 right hand drive **(type 116.05).** Chassis from AR11605*0001011 to *0001400.
2000 (type 115.36). Chassis from AR*2378451 to *2378863.
2000 right hand drive **(type 105.15).** Chassis from AR*2406638 to *2408105.
2000 Spider Veloce (type 115.38). Chassis from AR*2465781 to *2466550.
2000 Spider Veloce right hand drive **(type 105.27).** Chassis from AR*2472271 to *2472900.
2000 Spider Veloce injection America (type 115.02). Chassis from AR*3048901 to *3051363.
Montreal (type 105.64). Chassis included between AR*1428724 and *1428856.

COMPETITION CARS NOT FOR PUBLIC SALE:
MARTINI-BRABHAM-ALFA ROMEO BT 45 (BRABHAM-AUTODELTA) - SINGLE-SEATER FORMULA ONE CAR
MARTINI-BRABHAM-ALFA ROMEO BT 45 B (BRABHAM-AUTODELTA)- SINGLE-SEATER FORMULA ONE CAR
33/3 SC 12 (AUTODELTA) - TWO-SEATER SPORT FOR ROAD AND TRACK RACING
ALFASUD ti TROFEO (AUTODELTA PREPARATION KIT) - FOR TRACK RACING

ALFETTA 2000
(TYPE 116.55, ENGINE TYPE AR01623)

4 cylinders in line, 1962 cc, 122 hp, twin overhead camshafts. Wheelbase 2510 mm.

SALOON

With the introduction of the two litre engine, the entire car was updated with radical exterior modifications (radiator grill, headlights, bumpers, new door handles, rear lights) and internal changes (steering wheel, dashboard, seats, ventilation). **Chassis from AR11655*0001001 to *0030950.**

Alfetta 2.0 right hand drive (type 116.56). **Chassis from AR11656*3410001 to *3411540.**

ALFASUD ti 1.3
(TYPE 901G, ENGINE TYPE AR30184)

4 cylinders horizontally opposed, 1286 cc, 76 hp, 1 overhead camshaft per main bearing. Wheelbase 2455 mm.

SALOON

The Sprint's engine was installed in the ti, which produced a performance similar to that of the coupè. **Chassis from AS*5000001*901G to *5006499*901G.**

GIULIETTA 1.3
(TYPE 116.44, ENGINE TYPE AR01644)

4 cylinders in line, 1357 cc, 95 hp, twin overhead camshafts. Wheelbase 2510 mm.

**Chassis from AR11644*0001011
to *0004999.**

GIULIETTA 1.6
(TYPE 116.50, ENGINE TYPE AR01600)

4 cylinders in line, 1570 cc, 109 hp, twin overhead camshafts. Wheelbase 2510 mm.

**Chassis from AR11650*0001001
to *0003999.**

SALOON

The **Giulietta** name, which was used for a range of sensational cars throughout the Sixties, was used again for a radical updating of the **Alfetta**. The new car had a very attractive body with a little more space than its highly successful predecessor.

The characteristics of the 1.3 engine, with a stroke of just 67.5 mm and a bore of 80 mm, were similar to those of the **GTA 1300 Junior**; the 1.6 had a bore and stroke similar to the glorious Giulia, which was introduced in 1962.

Both cars became available in November.

ALFASUD 1.2 SUPER
(TYPE 901D, ENGINE TYPE 30102)
4 cylinders horizontally opposed, 1186 cc, 63 hp, 1 overhead camshaft
per main bearing. Wheelbase 2455 mm.

**Chassis from AS*5158900*901D
to *5217459*901D**

ALFASUD 1.3 SUPER
(TYPE 901F, ENGINE TYPE 30180)
4 cylinders horizontally opposed, 1286 cc, 68 hp, 1 overhead camshaft
per main bearing. Wheelbase 2455 mm.

**Chassis from AS*5000001*901F to
*5007200*901F.**

SALOON

The Super, with its two different engines, was presented in mid-December. The protection of the bodyshell was improved so that it became more corrosion resistant. The new **Alfasuds** were given new large bumpers with elasticised polypropylene protection and black radiator grill. The air intakes on the bonnet were also black, as were air outlets in the rear body pillars. The butterfly window frames were in stainless steel. The interior was completely new: updated seats, cloth inserts in the door panels and carpet on the floor; the dashboard was re-designed with two blue-faced circular instruments; on the transmission tunnel there was a small storage box; the steering wheel had three spokes with holes.

NO SIGNIFICANT MODIFICATIONS TO THE FOLLOWING MODELS:
Alfasud N (type 901D1), Alfasud 5 gear (type 901D). Chassis from AS*5158900*901D to *5217459*901D (in common with the Alfasud 1.2 Super). – **Alfasud ti (type 901C).** Chassis from AS*5454449*901C to *5469056* 901C. – **Alfasud Sprint (type 902A).** Chassis from AS*5006351*902A to *5017781*902A. – **Alfasud Giardinetta (type 904A).** Chassis in common with the type 904A1 – **Alfasud Giardinetta 5 speed (type 904A1).** Chassis from AS*5007001*904A to *5007077*904A, from AS*5007501*904A to *5008581*904A. – **Nuova Super 1.3 (type 115.09S).** Chassis from AR11509*0053051 to *0059583. – **Spider 1300 Junior (type 105.91S).** Chassis from AR10591*0002462 to *0002701. – **Nuova Super 1.6 (type 105.26S).** Chassis from AR10526*0020851 to *0028664.– **Spider 1600 Junior (type 115.35).** Chassis from AR11535*0001801 to *0002100. – **Alfetta 1.6 (type 116.00).** Chassis from AR11600*0050001 to *0062700. – **Alfetta 1.8 (type 116.42).** Chassis from AR*2152866 to *2158400. – **Alfetta right hand drive (type 116.09).** Chassis from AR*0008601 to *0009626. – **Alfetta GT 1.6 (type 116.04).** Chassis from AR11604*0004601 to *0005094. – **Alfetta GT 1.6** right hand drive **(type 116.02).** Chassis from AR11601*0005001 to *0005094. – **Alfetta GT 1.8** right hand drive **(type 116.05).** Chassis from AR11605*0001401 to *0002300. **Alfetta GTV 2000 (type 116.36).** Chassis from AR11636*0010951 to *0022650. – **Alfetta GTV 2000** right hand drive **(type 116.37)** Chassis from AR11637*0001901 to *0004200. **2000 Spider Veloce** (type 115.38). Chassis from AR11538*2466551 to *2467541. – **2000 Spider Veloce (type 115.38).** Chassis from AR*2466551 to *2467541 – **2000 Spider Veloce** right hand drive **(type 105.27).** Chassis from AR*2472901 to *2473095. – **2000 Spider Veloce injection America (type 115.02).** Chassis from AR*0001001 to *0001350. – **2000 Spider Veloce injection America (type 115.41).** Chassis from AR11541*0001001 to *0006000. – **Montreal (type 105.64).** Chassis included between AR*1428772 e *1428860.

COMPETITION CARS NOT FOR PUBLIC SALE:
MARTINI-BRABHAM-ALFA ROMEO BT 46 (BRABHAM-AUTODELTA) - SINGLE-SEATER FORMULA ONE CAR
33 SC 12 (AUTODELTA) - TWO-SEATER SPORT FOR ROAD AND TRACK RACING
33 SC 12 TURBO (CM³ 2134) (AUTODELTA) - TWO-SEATER SPORT FOR ROAD AND TRACK RACING
ALFASUD ti TROFEO (AUTODELTA PREPARATION KIT) - FOR TRACK RACING

ALFASUD ti 1.3
(TYPE 901G2, ENGINE TYPE AS30164)
4 cylinders opposed, 1351 cc, 79 hp, 1 overhead camshaft
per main bearing. Wheelbase 2455 mm.

**Chassis from AS*5015000*901G
to *5030600*901G.**

ALFASUD ti 1.5
(TYPE 901G1, ENGINE TYPE AS30124)
4 cylinders opposed, 1490 cc, 85 hp, 1 overhead camshaft
per main bearing. Wheelbase 2455 mm.

**Chassis from AS*5015000*901G
to *5030600*901G. (in common
with the ti 1.3)**

SALOON

New engines to take the place of the
old 1286 cc. There were the 1351
cc (increased stroke from 62 to 67.2
mm, bore unchanged) and the 1490
cc (bore and stroke 84 x 67.2 mm).
Minor modifications to the finish,
of which the most evident was a
new rear spoiler.

ALFASUD 1.5 SUPER
(TYPE 901F1, ENGINE TYPE AS30124)
4 cylinders opposed, 1490 cc, 85 hp, 1 overhead camshaft
per main bearing. Wheelbase 2455 mm.

SALOON

The four-door version of the ti 1.5.
The performance was high, with a
maximum speed of 165 km/h.
**Chassis from AS*5020001*901F to
*5040001*901F.**

ALFASUD SPRINT 1.3
(TYPE 902A3, ENGINE TYPE AS30164)

4 cylinders horizontally opposed, 1350 cc, 79 hp, 1 overhead camshaft
per main bearing. Wheelbase 2455 mm.

**Chassis from AS*5025000*902A
to *5039999*902A.**

ALFASUD SPRINT 1.5
(TYPE 902A1, ENGINE TYPE AS30124)

4 cylinders horizontally opposed, 1490 cc, 85 hp, 1 overhead camshaft
per main bearing. Wheelbase 2455 mm.

**Chassis from AS*5025000*902A
to *5039999*902A. (in common
with the ti 1.3)**

COUPE'

The new ti's engines were installed
in the new Sprint.
Maximum speeds 165 km/h and
170 km/h respectively.

ALFETTA 2000 L
(TYPE 116.55C, ENGINE TYPE AR01655)

4 cylinders in line, 1962 cc, 130 hp, twin overhead camshafts. Wheelbase 2510 mm.

SALOON

**Chassis from AR11655*0040001
to *0049600.**

At the beginning of July, interesting
modifications were revealed to
reduce fuel consumption, yet with
an 8 hp increase in power. This
was due to new camshafts which
raised the height of the valves from
9 mm to 9.5 mm and the new
pneumatic spark advance calibrator.
Outside, the only change was made
to the rear view mirror, while inside
the dashboard was covered with
briar while maintaining the same
lay-out. Later, the Alfetta 2000 L
was also offered with a sunroof.

ALFASUD 1.3 SUPER
(TYPE 901F2, ENGINE TYPE AS30160)

4 horizontally opposed cylinders, 1351 cc, 71 hp, 1 overhead camshaft per main bearing. Wheelbase 2455 mm.

SALOON

At the beginning of July, the 1351 cc engine was also adopted for the Super.
The carburettor was only a single choke and the compression ratio was low (9:1).
That was resolved with 8 hp less power than the ti and Sprint.
Chassis from AS*5020001*901F to *5040001*901F.

ALFASUD GIARDINETTA 1.3
(TYPE 904B, ENGINE TYPE AS30180)

4 cylinders horizontally opposed, 1286 cc, 68 hp, 1 overhead camshaft per main bearing. Wheelbase 2455 mm.

Chassis from AS*5001251*904B to *5001750*904B.

ALFASUD GIARDINETTA 1.3
(TYPE 904B2, ENGINE TYPE AS30160)

4 cylinders horizontally opposed, 1351 cc, 71 hp, 1 overhead camshaft per main bearing. Wheelbase 2455 mm.

Chassis in common with type 904 B.

STATION WAGON

During the year, the Giardinetta underwent the normal evolution modifications of the saloon, adopting the Super's type 30160 engine of the 1.3 Super.

ALFETTA 2.0 AMERICA
(TYPE 116.58, ENGINE TYPE AR01615)

4 cylinders in line, 1962 cc, 111 hp, twin overhead camshafts. Wheelbase 2510 mm.

SALOON

The America version of the **Alfetta** was given Spica mechanical injection. Power dropped noticeably to the advantage of fuel consumption and a more uniform drive quality. The car also became available with an automatic gearbox: ZF type 3 HP 22 transmission and three speeds with torque converter.
An auto-blocking differential at 25% was also on the way as original equipment.
Chassis from AR11658*0001011 to *0002992.

ALFETTA GTV 2000 L
(TYPE 116.36A, ENGINE TYPE AR01655)
4 cylinders in line, 1962 cc, 130 hp, twin overhead camshafts. Wheelbase 2400 mm.

COUPE'

The coupè adopted the **Alfetta 2000 L** saloon's engine and a different suspension rating. Maximum speed 195 km/h.
Chassis from AR11636*0030001 to *0034000.

NO SIGNIFICANT MODIFICATIONS TO THE FOLLOWING MODELS:
Alfasud N (type 901D1), Alfasud 1.2 Super (type 901D). Chassis from AS*5270153*901D to *5295800*901D.
Alfasud 1.3 Super (type 901F). Chassis from AS*007201*901F to *5040000*901F
Alfasud ti 1.3 (type 901G). Chassis from AS*5006500*901G to *5030600*901G.
Alfasud Sprint 1.3 (type 902A). Chassis from AS*5017781*902A to *5024999*902A.
Giulietta 1.3 (type 116.44). Chassis from AR11644*0005000 to *0025500.
Giulietta 1.6 (type 116.50). Chassis from AR11650*0004000 to *0033999.
Alfetta 1.6 (type 116.00). Chassis from AR*0062701 to *0070100.
Alfetta GT 1.6 (type 116.04). Chassis from AR*0012351 to *0015004.
Alfetta 1.8 (type 116.42). Chassis from AR*2158401 to *2166239.
Alfetta right hand drive **(type 116.09).** Chassis from AR*0009627 to *0009866.
Alfetta GT 1.8 right hand drive **(type 116.05).** Chassis from AR*0002301 to *0002540.
Alfetta 2000 (type 116.55). Chassis from AR*0030951 to *0035733.
Alfetta 2000 right hand drive **(type 116.56).** Chassis from AR*0001001 to *0002561, from AR*0003001 to *0004300.
Alfetta GTV 2000 (type 116.36). Chassis from AR*0022651 to *0027099.
Alfetta GTV 2000 right hand drive **(type 116.37).** Chassis from AR*0004201 to *0005050, from AR*0010001 to *0011800.
Spider 1600 (type 115.35). Chassis from AR*0002101 to *0002999, from ZAR115350*00003001 to *00003199.
2000 Spider Veloce (type 115.38). Chassis from AR11538*2467542 to *24669100.
2000 Spider Veloce injection America (type 115.41). Chassis from AR11541*0006001 to *0006400.

COMPETITION CARS NOT FOR PUBLIC SALE
MARTINI-BRABHAM-ALFA ROMEO BT 46 (BRABHAM-AUTODELTA) - SINGLE-SEATER FORMULA ONE CAR
177 (AUTODELTA) - SINGLE-SEATER FORMULA ONE CAR
33/3 SC 12 (AUTODELTA) - TWO-SEATER SPORT FOR ROAD AND TRACK RACING
ALFASUD ti TROFEO (AUTODELTA PREPARATION KIT) - FOR TRACK RACING

GIULIETTA 1.8
(TYPE 116A, ENGINE TYPE AR01678)
4 cylinders in line, 1779 cc, 122 hp, twin overhead camshafts. Wheelbase 2510 mm.

SALOON

The new rendering of the **Giulietta** was fitted with an optimised version of the **1750** engine.
Due to the extra torque, a long ratio was adopted (10/41) which ensured a noticeable increase in top speed (180 km/h) at relatively low engine revs.
Maximum power (122 hp DIN) was obtained at 5300 rpm.
Fuel consumption was in line with the 1.6.
Chassis from AR116A*0001011 to *0004000; from ZAR116A00*00004001 to *00015800.

ALFASUD 1.3 SUPER
(TYPE 901F3, ENGINE TYPE AS30164)
4 cylinders horizontally opposed, 1351 cc, 71 hp, 1 overhead camshaft per main bearing. Wheelbase 2455 mm.

Chassis from ZAS901F30*05066000 to 05071000.

ALFASUD 1.5 SUPER
(TYPE 901F4, ENGINE TYPE AS30124)
4 cylinders horizontally opposed, 1490 cc, 85 hp, 1 overhead camshaft per main bearing. Wheelbase 2455 mm.

Chassis from ZAS901F40*05066000 to *05071000.

SALOON

This version of the Alfasud saloon adopted the 1.5 ti engine. It almost had the performance of a sports car, with a maximum speed of 165 km/h. The 1.3 was given a twin-choke carburettor.

ALFA 6

(TYPE 119A, ENGINE TYPE ARO1913)
(five speed mechanical gearbox plus reverse)

Chassis from AR119A*0001011 to *0001999, from ZAR119A00*00002001 to *00003699.

ALFA 6

(TYPE 119A1, ENGINE TYPE ARO1913)
(ZF automatic gearbox with three forward gears and a reverse)

V6 at 60°, 2492 cc, 160 hp, 1 overhead camshaft per main bearing. Wheelbase 2600 mm.

Chassis from AR119A*2001001 to *2001200, from ZAR119A10*02001201 to *02001299.

SALOON

Even if it was late – the **Alfa 6** project goes back as far as that of the Alfetta – Alfa Romeo's top-of-the-range car arrived eventually. Planned for 1973, it's debut was halted by the energy crisis and the car went on sale six years later.
Its performance was notable due to the amount of test driving carried out by Alfa's most expert test drivers, who were able to instill into this production model qualities typical of a racing car. Top speed 200 km/h, surprising roadholding (De Dion rear axle) in any road conditions. Like many other Alfa Romeos, the **Alfa 6** became well-known as a car which "forgave" driving errors.
It became the most powerful of all Italian saloons and the only one

with a six cylinder engine.

_ ALFETTA GTV 2.0 TURBODELTA _

(TYPE 116.36D, ENGINE TYPE AR01655)

4 cylinders in line, 1962 cc, 150 hp, twin overhead camshafts. Wheelbase 2400 mm.

COUPE'

The first Italian car manufacturer to use a turbocharger on a petrol-driven production car was Alfa Romeo.
The **Alfetta GTV 2000 Turbodelta** was developed by Autodelta, Alfa Romeo's racing department, and exploited the experience of the Settimo Milanese company.
Made by KKK, the turbocharger was completely modified to ensure the materials of which the turbine was made could withstand the extremely high temperatures at which it "worked" (around 1000°). Normal **Alfetta GTV 2000 L** type 116.36A cars were taken from production and sent to Autodelta, where the engine and bonnet were replaced with those of the racing department.
Chassis included in the Alfetta GTV 2000 L numbering system.

ALFASUD SPRINT VELOCE 1.3
(TYPE 902A4, ENGINE TYPE AS30168)

4 cylinders horizontally opposed, 1351 cc, 86 hp, 1 overhead camshaft
per main bearing. Wheelbase 2455 mm.

**Chassis from ZAS902A40*05046000
to *05055600.**

ALFASUD SPRINT VELOCE 1.5
(TYPE 902A5, ENGINE TYPE AS30128)

4 cylinders horizontally opposed, 1490 cc, 95 hp, 1 overhead camshaft
per main bearing. Wheelbase 2455 mm.

**Chassis from ZAS902A50*05046000
to *05055600.**

COUPE'

This car's appearance was identical to the previous version's except for the rear script, while the mechanical characteristics were particularly exciting.
The carburettors were two twin chokes which, together with the compression ratio and a different timing of the camshafts, increased the power of the 1.3 by 9% and the 1.5 by 12%.
So individual fuel supply (one carburettor per cylinder) had even come to the **Alfasud**, after being extensively tested on racing cars and introduced for the first time on a production car with the **1900 T.I.** in 1951.

ALFASUD ti 1.3
(TYPE 901G4, ENGINE TYPE AS30168)

4 cylinders horizontally opposed, 1351 cc, 86 hp, 1 overhead camshaft
per main bearing. Wheelbase 2455 mm.

ALFASUD ti 1.5
(TYPE 901G5, ENGINE TYPE AR30128)

4 cylinders horizontally opposed, 1490 cc, 95 hp, 1 overhead camshaft
per main bearing. Wheelbase 2455 mm.

SALOON

The Sprint and Sprint Veloce engines also equipped the ti.

Performance was even superior to the coupè, because the saloon was lighter and more aerodynamic. Fittings were updated in line with the third series.

**Chassis from ZAS901G40*05051405
to *05052300 (for both models).**

ALFETTA TURBO DIESEL

(TYPE 116B, ENGINE TYPE 4HT/2)

4 cylinders in line, 1995 cc, 82 hp, 1 camshaft in crankcase. Wheelbase 2510 mm.

SALOON

After the uninspiring performance of the **Giulia Diesel**, Alfa Romeo finally entered the diesel market in style with a car whose performance was equal to a 1600 cc petrol engined saloon.
Chassis from ZAR116B00*00001001 to ZAR116B00*00001350.

NO SIGNIFICANT MODIFICATIONS TO THE FOLLOWING MODELS:

Alfasud N (type 901D1), Alfasud 1.2 Super (type 901 D). Chassis from AS*5295801*901D to *5324999*901D. from ZAS901D00*05235000 to ZAS901D00*05331400.
Alfasud 1.3 Super (type 901F2). Chassis from AS*5040002*901F to *5065999*901F.
Alfasud ti 1.5 (type 901G1). Chassis from AS*5030601*901G to *5049999*901G, from ZAS901G10*05050000 to *05051404.
Alfasud 1.5 Super (type 901F1). Chassis from AS*5040002*901F to *5065999*901F.
Alfasud Giardinetta 1.3 (type 904B2). Numbers not available after AS*904B20*05003001.
Alfasud ti 1.3 (type 901G). Chassis from AS*5030601*901G to *5049999*901G, from ZAS901G20*05050000 to *05051404
Alfasud ti 1.3 (type 901G2). Chassis from AS*5030601*901G to *5049999*901G, from ZAS901G20*05050000 to *05051404.
Alfasud Sprint 1.3 (type 902A3). Chassis from AS*5040000*902A to *5045999*902A.
Alfasud ti 1.5 (type 901G1). Chassis from AS*5030601*901G to *5049999, from ZAS901G10*05050000 to *05051404.
Alfasud Sprint 1.5 (type 902A1). Chassis from AS*5040000*902A to *5045999*902A.
Giulietta 1.3 (type 116.44). Chassis from AR11644*0025501 to *0037900.
Giulietta 1.6 (type 116.50). Chassis from AR11650*0034000 to *0069200.
Alfetta 1.6 (type 116.00). Chassis from AR11600*0070101 to *0076100.
Alfetta GT 1.6 (type 116.04). Chassis from AR11604*0015005 to *0015799.
Alfetta 1.8 (type 116.42). Chassis from AR*2170001 to *2170600.
Alfetta 2000 L (type 116.55C). Chassis from AR11655*0049601 to *0072500.
Alfetta 2.0 America (type 116.58). Chassis from AR11658*0002993 to *0003600.
Alfetta GTV 2000 (type 116.36A). Chassis from AR11636*0034001 to *0041000.
Spider 1600 (type 115.35). Chassis from ZAR115350*00003200 to *0003600.
2000 Spider Veloce (type 115.38). Chassis from AR11538*2469101 to *2471099.
2000 Spider Veloce injection America (type 115.41). Chassis from AR11541*0006401 to *0009101.

COMPETITION CARS NOT FOR PUBLIC SALE
MARTINI-BRABHAM-ALFA ROMEO BT 48 (BRABHAM-AUTODELTA) (V 12 AT 60°) SINGLE-SEATER FORMULA ONE CAR
177 (AUTODELTA) - SINGLE-SEATER FORMULA ONE CAR
179 (AUTODELTA) - SINGLE-SEATER FORMULA ONE CAR
ALFASUD ti TROFEO (AUTODELTA PREPARATION KIT) - FOR TRACK RACING

1980

ALFASUD 1.2 SUPER
(TYPE 901D5, ENGINE TYPE AS30102)
(4 speed, twin-choke carburettor)
4 cylinders horizontally opposed, 1186 cc, 63 hp, 1 overhead camshaft per main bearing. Wheelbase 2455 mm.

Chassis from ZAS901D50*05331401 to *05370500.

ALFASUD 1.2 SUPER
(TYPE 901D4, ENGINE TYPE AS30104)
(5-speed, twin-choke carburettor)
4 cylinders horizontally opposed, 1186 cc, 68 hp, 1 overhead camshaft per main bearing. Wheelbase 2455 mm.

Chassis from ZAS901D40*05331401 to *05370500 (in common with the 4-speed version).

ALFASUD 1.3 SUPER
(TYPE 901F3, ENGINE TYPE AS30164)
4 cylinders horizontally opposed, 1351 cc, 71 hp, 1 overhead camshaft per main bearing. Wheelbase 2455 mm.

Chassis from ZAS901F30*05071001 to *05096046.

ALFASUD 1.3 SUPER
(TYPE 901F3A, ENGINE TYPE AS30164)
4 cylinders horizontally opposed, 1351 cc, 79 hp, 1 overhead camshaft per main bearing. Wheelbase 2455 mm.

With type 901F3A, the engine type AS30164 was given two twin-choke carburettors and the car's power increased by 8 hp.
Chassis from ZAS901F30*05096047 to *05100999.

ALFASUD 1.5
(TYPE 901F4, ENGINE TYPE AS30124)

4 cylinders horizontally opposed, 1490 cc, 85 hp, 1 overhead camshaft per main bearing. Wheelbase 2455 mm.

Chassis from ZAS901F40*05071001 to *05096046.

ALFASUD 1.5
(TYPE 901F4A, ENGINE TYPE AS30124)

4 cylinders horizontally opposed, 1490 cc, 85 hp, 1 overhead camshaft per main bearing. Wheelbase 2455 mm.

Chassis from ZAS901F40*05096047 to *05100999.

ALFASUD ti 1.3
(TYPE 901G4, ENGINE TYPE AS30168)

4 cylinders horizontally opposed, 1351 cc, 79 hp, 1 overhead camshaft per main bearing. Wheelbase 2455 mm.

Chassis from ZAS901G40*05052301 to *05063300.

Alfasud ti 1.3-1.5.

ALFASUD ti 1.5
(TYPE 901G5, ENGINE TYPE AS30128)

4 cylinders horizontally opposed, 1490 cc, 85 hp, 1 overhead camshaft per main bearing. Wheelbase 2455 mm.

Chassis from ZAS901G50*05052301 to *05063300 (in common with the 1.3 ti)

SALOON

All third series Alfasuds were given a complete re-styling, which was necessary eight years after its introduction. New bumper bars, new radiator grill, stylised badges in relief on the rear pillars and black handles; tail lights which extended to the boot lid; no more chrome edging for the tail. The Giulietta's wheels were fitted. Inside: a more modern dashboard, bigger front seats, new door panels with handles in imitation wood. Engine power was increased, except for the 4-speed versions. Tubeless tyres.

ALFETTA 1.8
(TYPE 116.42A, ENGINE TYPE ARO1678)

4 cylinders in line, 1779 cc, 122 hp, twin overhead camshafts. Wheelbase 2510 mm.

SALOON

The car returned to the first

Alfetta's 1975 power output which, with type 116.42, was reduced to 118 hp.
Chassis from ZAR116420*02171001

to *02173499.

SPIDER VELOCE 1600
(TYPE 115.35, ENGINE TYPE AR00526A*S)

4 cylinders in line, 1570 cc, 102 hp, twin overhead camshafts. Wheelbase 2250 mm.

PININFARINA ROADSTER

An alternative to the **2000 Spider Veloce**, this was a more economical but still high performance version. Top speed 175 km/h.
Chassis from ZAR115350*00004001 to *00004750.

GTV 6 2.5
(TYPE 116C, ENGINE TYPE AR01646)

V6 at 60°, 2492 cc, 160 hp, 1 overhead camshaft per main bearing.
Wheelbase 2400 mm.

COUPE'

The GTV 6 was born of the happy marriage between the **Alfetta GT** and the engine of the **Alfa 6**, but with fuel injection. The result was a prestigious car, the racing version of which also brought Alfa Romeo numerous successes.

Many modifications, some of which also extended to the GT; updated dashboard with principal instrumentation grouped together in front of the driver; black plastic bumpers; many details in black, such as the plastic element which joins together the lower side panel to the wheel housing, the edges of

the small windows and the air intakes on the bonnet. The latter provided a protrusion which permitted the accommodation of the bigger engine.
Chassis from ZAR116C00*00001001 to *00006000 (including some cars made in 1981).
1980 production was of cars which were predominantly not registered for sale but "charged to internal units". In other words cars for company use, including competition.

GIULIETTA SUPER

(TYPE 116A1, ENGINE TYPE AR01655)

4 cylinders in line, 1962 cc, 130 hp, twin overhead camshafts. Wheelbase 2510 mm.

SALOON

A Giulietta with a two litre engine had been sold overseas for some time, but there were doubts about making it available to the home market as it may have penalised the satisfactory sales of the Alfetta, which was still popular. The decision to go ahead was eventually taken in 1980. The new car was distinguished by its mono-colour of metallic grey and many details in matt black. A thin grey stripe ran along the length of the body. Double external rear vision mirrors and new wheels for 185/65 HR 14 tyres. Inside, a new steering wheel and beaver coloured seats with a beige stripe which matched the external beige body line.

Chassis from ZAR116A10*00001001 to*00008010.

NO SIGNIFICANT MODIFICATIONS TO THE FOLLOWING MODELS:
Alfasud Giardinetta 1.3 (type 904B2). Chassis: numbers not available.
Alfasud Sprint Veloce 1.3 (type 902A4). Chassis from ZAS902A40*05055601 to *05070000.
Alfasud Sprint Veloce 1.5 (type 902A5). Chassis from ZAS902A50*05055601 to *05070000.
Giulietta 1.3 (type 116.44). Chassis from AR11644*0037901 to *0038500, from ZAR116440*00038501 to *00045400.
Giulietta 1.6 (type 116.50). Chassis from AR11650*0069201 to *0072000, from ZAR116500*00072001 to *00099951.
Giulietta 1.8 (type 116A). Chassis from ZAR116A00*00015801 to *00030900.
Alfetta 1.6 (type 116.00). Chassis from 0076151 to 0076950, from ZAR116000*00076201 to *00081900.
Alfetta GT 1.6 (type 116.04). Chassis from AR11604*0015800 to *0016450.
Alfetta 1.8 (type 116.42). Chassis from AR*2170601 to *2171000.
Alfetta 2000 L (type 116.55C). Chassis from AR11655*0072501 to *0073999, from ZAR116550*00074001 to *00100100.
Alfetta GTV 2000 L (type 116.36A). Chassis from AR11636*0041001 to *0044000.
Alfetta GTV 2000 L (type 116.36B). Chassis from ZAR116360*00050001 to *00050600.
Alfetta GTV 2.0 Turbodelta (*) (type 116.36D). Chassis included in the **Alfetta GTV 2000 L** numbering system.
Alfetta Turbo Diesel (type 116B). Chassis from ZAR116B00*00001351 to *00005180.
Alfa 6 (type 119A). Chassis from ZAR119A00*00003700 to *00005900.
Alfa 6 (type 119A1). Chassis from ZAR119A10*02001300 to *02001999.
2000 Spider Veloce (type 115.38). Chassis from AR11538*2471100 to *2474700.
2000 Spider Veloce injection America (type 115.41). Chassis from AR11541*0010001 to *0011202.

(*) **Cars were taken from Alfetta GTV 2.0 L (type 116.36A) production and elaborated by Autodelta.**

COMPETITION CARS NOT FOR PUBLIC SALE
179 (AUTODELTA) - SINGLE-SEATER FORMULA ONE CAR
ALFASUD ti TROFEO (AUTODELTA PREPARATION KIT) - FOR TRACK RACING

1981

ALFASUD 1.2 SUPER

(TYPE 901D4A, ENGINE TYPE AS30104)
(normal ratios)

Chassis from ZAS901D40*05370501
to *05419000.

ALFASUD 1.2 SUPER

(TYPE 901D4C, ENGINE TYPE AS30104)
(long ratios)

Chassis from ZAS901D40*05419001
to *05447750.

4 cylinders horizontally opposed, 1186 cc, 68 hp, 1 overhead camshaft per main bearing. Wheelbase 2455 mm.

ALFASUD 1.3 SUPER

(TYPE 901F3A, ENGINE TYPE AS30164)
(2 twin-choke carburettors, 3 doors)

Chassis from ZAS901F30*05101000
to *05127999.

ALFASUD 1.3 SUPER

(TYPE 901F3B, ENGINE TYPE AS30164)
(2 twin-choke carburettors, 4 doors, long ratios)

Chassis from ZAS901F30*05128000
to *05135300.

4 cylinders horizontally opposed, 1351 cc, 79 cc, 1 overhead camshaft per main bearing. Wheelbase 2455 mm.

ALFASUD 1.5

(TYPE 901F4A, ENGINE TYPE AS30124)
(normal ratios)

Chassis from ZAS901F40*05101000
to *05127999.

ALFASUD 1.5

(TYPE 901F4B, ENGINE TYPE AS30124)
(long ratios)

Chassis from ZAS901F40*05128000
to *05135300.

4 cylinders horizontally opposed, 1490 cc, 85 hp, 1 overhead camshaft per main bearing. Wheelbase 2455 mm.

ALFASUD ti 1.3
(TYPE 901G4A, ENGINE TYPE AS30168)
(normal ratios)

Chassis from ZAS901G40*05066001
to *05076999.

ALFASUD ti 1.3
(TYPE 901G4B, ENGINE TYPE AS30168)
(long ratios)

Chassis from ZAS901G40*05077000
to *05080900.

4 cylinders horizontally opposed, 1351 cc, 86 hp, 1 overhead camshaft per main bearing. Wheelbase 2455 mm.

ALFASUD ti 1.5
(TYPE 901G5A, ENGINE TYPE AS30128)
(normal ratios)

Chassis from ZAS901G50*05066001
to *05076999.

ALFASUD ti 1.5
(TYPE 901G5B, ENGINE TYPE AS30128)
(long ratios)

Chassis from ZAS901G50*05077000
to *05080900.

4 cylinders horizontally opposed, 1490 cc, 95 hp, 1 overhead camshaft per main bearing. Wheelbase 2455 mm.

SALOON

This 1981 **Alfasud**, available with a hatchback was a 3 door. A 4 door version was not made.
The introduction of the hatchback required a number of structural modifications which increased the car's weight by 25 kg, among them a rear cross member to improve torsional resistance.
The ti also had *breakerless* electronic ignition.
The C and B series had long ratios.

NUOVA GIULIETTA L 1.3
(TYPE 116.44, ENGINE TYPE AR01644)

4 cylinders in line, 1357 cc, 95 hp, twin overhead camshafts. Wheelbase 2510 mm.

**Chassis fromZAR116440*00050001
to*00056499.**

NUOVA GIULIETTA L 1.6
(TYPE 116.50B, ENGINE TYPE AR01600)

4 cylinders in line, 1570 cc, 109 hp, twin overhead camshafts. Wheelbase 2510 mm.

**Chassis from ZAR116500*00000051
to*00136300.**

NUOVA GIULIETTA L 1.8
(TYPE 116AA, ENGINE TYPE AR01678)

4 cylinders in line, 1779 cc, 122 hp, twin overhead camshafts. Wheelbase 2510 mm.

**Chassis from ZAR116A00*00030901
to *00044500 (including type 116 A).**

SALOON

Available from the second half of June, the second series Giulietta had a new look. Many of the car's details were revised and, compared to the 2.0, the coloured stripe which encircled the body was lowered to bumper height.

The side panels of the 1.8 had ample plastic protection which ran along its length below the doors, while the 1.3 and 1.6 had a simpler molding to protect the car from blows.

Lock separate from the door handle and new design of the air outlet grills on the rear pillars.

The second series Giulietta also had a new identification script on the tail and fog lights fitted to the bumpers.

Many modifications to the interior, too: re-designed steering wheel, seats, instruments and central glove box which extended to the gear lever.

Same performance as the previous series.

ALFASUD SPRINT PLUS

(TYPE 902A5, ENGINE TYPE AS30128)

4 cylinders horizontally opposed, 1490 cc, 95 hp, 1 overhead camshaft per main bearing. Wheelbase 2455 mm.

COUPE'

Plus sales began in early July. The car differed from the normal versions by its external decoration and better internal furnishings. Only available in metallic bronze with a gold coloured self-adhesive stripe. Alloy wheels planned.

Steering wheel finished in imitation wood and seats in velvet, like the GTV.
Total production was 2,000 cars, of which only 700 were sold in Italy. **Chassis included between ZAS902A50*05070001 and *05079999.**

ALFETTA 1.6

(TYPE 116B1A, ENGINE TYPE ARO1600)

4 cylinders in line, 1570 cc, 109 hp, twin overhead camshafts. Wheelbase 2510 mm.

Chassis from ZAR116B10*00001001 to *00001900.

ALFETTA 1.8

(TYPE 116B2, ENGINE TYPE AR01678)

4 cylinders in line, 1779 cc, 122 hp, twin overhead camshafts. Wheelbase 2510 mm

Chassis from ZAR116B20*00001001 to *00001850.

ALFETTA 2.0

(TYPE 116.55F, ENGINE TYPE AR01655)

4 cylinders in line, 1962 cc, 130 hp, twin overhead camshafts. Wheelbase 2510 mm.

Chassis from ZAR116550*00100101 to *00121100.

ALFETTA TURBO DIESEL
(TYPE 116B, ENGINE TYPE 4HT2)
4 cylinders in line, 1995 cc, 1 camshaft in crankcase. Wheelbase 2510 mm.

Chassis from ZAR116B00*00005181 to *00011600, from ZAR116B00*00013001 to *00014050.

SALOON

Planned for 1982, modifications to the different versions of the **Alfetta** were announced in December.
By this time, the bodyshell was common to all four versions but the most significant modifications were made to the **Alfetta** 2.0, which was given an opaque aluminium radiator grill and headlight washers. The hub caps were black, the door mirrors could be adjusted electrically and the lateral indicator repeaters were further back. Interior coverings were also new, as were the conformation of the seats and de-frosting vents.
Other versions differed in other detail: no electric windows (only standard on the Turbo Diesel) while preparation was made for the fitment of headlight washers; headrests and rear seat belts.
The only mechanical change was different gear ratios, which reduced consumption by 3%.

NO SIGNIFICANT MODIFICATIONS TO THE FOLLOWING CARS:
Alfasud ti 1.3 (type 901G4). Chassis from ZAS901G40*05063301 to *05066000.
Alfasud Giardinetta 1.3 (type 904B2). Chassis: numbers not available.
Alfasud Sprint Veloce 1.3 (type 902A4). Chassis from ZAS902A40*05070001 to *05079999.
Alfasud Sprint Veloce 1.3 (type 902A4A) (long ratios). Chassis from ZAS902A40*05080000 to *05089999.
Alfasud ti 1.5 (type 901 G5). Chassis from ZAS901G40*05066999 (partially in common with the ti 1.3).
Alfasud Sprint Veloce 1.5 (type 902A5). Chassis from ZAS902A50*05070001 to *05079999.
Alfasud Sprint Veloce 1.5 (type 902A5A) (long ratios). Chassis from ZAS902A50*05080000 to *05089999.
Giulietta 1.3 (type 116.44). Chassis from ZAR116440*00045401 to *00047300.
Nuova Giulietta L 2.0 (type 116A1A). Chassis from ZAR116A10*00008011 to* 00017000 (including type 116 A1).
Alfetta 1.6 (type 116.00). Chassis from ZAR116000*00081901 to *00082800.
Alfetta 2.0 America (type 116.58B). Chassis from ZAR116580*00004001 to *00005250.
Alfetta GTV 2000 (type 116.36B). Chassis from ZAR116360*00050601 to *00055100.
Alfetta GTV 2.0 Turbodelta (*)(type 116.36D). Chassis included in the **Alfetta GTV 2000 L** numbering system.
Alfa 6 (type 119A), (type 119A1). No cars produced.
GTV 6 2.5 (type 116C). Chassis from ZAR116C00*00007501 to *00008000.
GTV 6 2.5 with catalytic converter for the U.S.A. market **(type 116.69, engine type 01911).**
     Chassis from ZAR116690*00001001 onwards.
1600 Spider Veloce (type 115.35). Chassis from ZAR115350*00004751 to *00004999.
2000 Spider Veloce (type 115.38). Chassis from AR11538*2474701 to *2475000, from ZAR115380*02475001 to *02475200.
2000 Spider Veloce injection America (type 115.41). Chassis from ZAR115410*00012601 to *00013059.

**(*) Cars taken from the Alfetta GTV production
2.0 L (116.36A) elaborated by Autodelta.**

COMPETITION CARS NOT FOR PUBLIC SALE
179 (AUTODELTA) - SINGLE-SEATER FORMULA ONE CAR
ALFASUD ti TROFEO (AUTODELTA PREPARATION KIT) - FOR TRACK RACING.

ALFASUD JUNIOR
(TYPE 901D4B, ENGINE TYPE AS30104)
4 cylinders horizontally opposed, 1186 cc, 68 hp, 1 overhead camshaft
per main bearing. Wheelbase 2455 mm.

SALOON

A special series (6000 cars in total, of which 4500 for the Italian market) of the five-speed, four door **Alfasud 1.2** which was offered at Lit 650,000 less than the standard 1.2 five-speed due to substantial simplification of the interior. Externally, the car had a three-colour (red, orange and yellow) stripe which ran along the sides above the upper door molding and boot lid script.
Engine numbers began at 5000001.
Chassis from ZAS901D40*05419001 to*05447750.

ALFASUD SPRINT VELOCE 1.5 TROFEO
(TYPE 902A5A, ENGINE TYPE AS30128)
4 cylinders horizontally opposed, 1490 cc, 95 hp, 1 overhead camshaft
per main bearing. Wheelbase 2455 mm.

COUPE'

In 1982, the Sprint Veloce also competed in the **Alfasud** Trophy racing series (Trofeo Alfasud) and to celebrate that fact a few coupès named Trofeo were built.
Body colour was metallic grey with a darker grey stripe running along the side, towards the back of which the name Trofeo was incorporated. Wheels were light alloy with stylised spokes for 165/70 SR 13 tyres.
Chassis from ZAS902A50*05090000 to *05092200.

ALFASUD 1.3 SUPER
(TYPE 901F3C, ENGINE TYPE AS30164)
(3 doors, long ratios)

4 cylinders horizontally opposed, 1351 cc, 79 hp, 1 overhead camshaft per main bearing. Wheelbase 2455 mm.

SALOON

Three-door version with long ratio gears, an alternative to type 901 F3B with its four doors and long ratios.
Chassis from ZAS901F30*05136913 to*05170000.

ALFASUD 1.2 S and 1.2 SC
(TYPE 901D4D, ENGINE TYPE AS30104)

4 cylinders horizontally opposed, 1186 cc, 68 hp, 1 overhead camshaft per main bearing. Wheelbase 2455 mm.

Chassis from ZAS901D40*05419001 to*05447750.

ALFASUD 1.3 SC
(TYPE 901F3D, ENGINE TYPE AS30164)

4 cylinders horizontally opposed, 1351 cc, 79 hp, 1 overhead camshaft per main bearing. Wheelbase 2455 mm.

Chassis from ZAS901F30*05137865 to*05170000.

ALFASUD 1.5
(TYPE 901F4C, ENGINE TYPE AS30124)

4 cylinders horizontally opposed, 1490 cc, 85 hp, 1 overhead camshaft per main bearing. Wheelbase 2455 mm.

Chassis from ZAS901F40*05136916 to *05170000.

ALFASUD 1.5 QUADRIFOGLIO ORO
(TYPE 901F4D, ENGINE TYPE AS30128)

4 cylinders horizontally opposed, 1490 cc, 95 hp, 1 overhead camshaft per main bearing. Wheelbase 2455 mm.

Chasis from ZAS901F40*5137865 to *05170000 (in common with model 1.3 SC).

SALOON

The four-door version was discontinued in May except for the 1.2 (901D4B) and was substituted by the five-door. The S and SC (Super and Super Comfort) versions were introduced, the only difference between the two being the interior finish. All the saloons were equipped with a five-speed, longer ratio gearbox which reduced fuel consumption (average 13.5% on the 1.3).
Included as original equipment were: headlight washers, rear window wiper, grey radiator grill with shiny Alfa Romeo shield and grey bumper.
The top-of-the-range Quadrifoglio Oro also had electric windows, different seat covering, new steering wheel and armrests in imitation wood.

ALFASUD 1.2 JUNIOR
(TYPE 901D4B, ENGINE TYPE AS30104)

4 cylinders horizontally opposed, 1186 cc, 63 hp, 1 overhead camshaft per main bearing. Wheelbase 2455 mm.

SALOON

The only **Alfasud** to retain four doors, but as an option, was also available with a hatchback in S and SC finish. Power and performance were unchanged but, with the introduction of the five-speed gearbox and longer ratios, fuel consumption was reduced by 11.4%.
Chassis from ZAS901D40*05419001 to*05447750.

ALFASUD 1.3 SC
(TYPE 901F3C, ENGINE TYPE AS30164)

4 cylinders horizontally opposed, 1351 cc, 79 hp, 1 overhead camshaft per main bearing. Wheelbase 2455 mm.

SALOON

The only three-door to remain in production; offered as an alternative to the five-door.
Same modifications: five-speed gearbox and a reduction in fuel consumption.
Chassis from ZAS901F30*05136913 to *05170000.

ALFETTA QUADRIFOGLIO
(TYPE 116.55M, ENGINE TYPE AR01334)
4 cylinders in line, 1962 cc, 128 hp, twin overhead camshafts. Wheelbase 2510 mm.

SALOON

After the **Alfasud**, the **Alfetta** also wore the company's sporting motif, the four leaf clover.
Performance and mechanical characteristics were unchanged.
The car had four headlights, light alloy wheels and bumper, under-door strip, headlight rims and radiator grill, all in brown.
Among the instruments was a nine function check system which included oil and brake liquid levels, various warning lights and correct door closure.
Chassis from ZAR116550*00145011 to*00145013.

ALFETTA QUADRIFOGLIO ORO
(TYPE 116.58C, ENGINE TYPE AR01674)
4 cylinders in line, 1962 cc, 125 hp, twin overhead camshafts. Wheelbase 2510 mm.

SALOON

Spica electronic ignition was fitted to this model, which became similar to that exported to the U.S.A.
Chassis from ZAR116580*00006011 to*00008810.

GIULIETTA 2.0 Ti

(TYPE 116A1A, ENGINE TYPE ARO1655)

4 cylinders in line, 1962 cc, 130 hp, twin overhead camshafts. Wheelbase 2510 mm.

SALOON

Produced as a limited edition, this car boasted several innovations in its external and internal finish. Lateral molding in grey metallic paint, the guttering was in black. Brown tinted glass with dark rubber draught excluders but no edging for the windscreen or rear window. The wheels were in magnesium alloy with Pirelli P6 tyres size 185/65 HR 14.
Inside, the steering wheel rim was covered in grey leather with the company badge in the centre, electronic speedometer and rev counter, electric front windows, seats covered in cloth and imitation leather.
The engine was the **Alfetta**'s reliable two litre.

Chassis included between ZAR116A10*00017001 and *00021650.

ALFASUD ti 1.5 QUADRIFOGLIO VERDE

(TYPE 901G5C, ENGINE TYPE AS30146)

4 cylinders horizontally opposed, 1490 cc, 105 hp, 1 overhead camshaft per main bearing. Wheelbase 2455 mm.

SALOON

From the introduction of this model onwards, Alfa Romeo branded all its sportier cars with the prestigious four leaf clover symbol, adopted by the company after its victory in the 1923 Targa Florio. The first car to wear the sporting emblem was the **Alfasud ti 1.5**, the power of which was increased with modifications that included a camshaft with higher performance timing. Maximum speed was over 180 km/h and acceleration was lively.
Few aesthetic modifications: a small wing on the hatchback, front shield bordered in red, light alloy wheels with eight holes and 190/55 HR 340 TRX or P6 185/60 HR 14 tyres.
Black edgings and guttering.
Inside, the steering wheel rim was covered in leather, the central panel of the seats was in cloth interwoven with the ti script.
Chassis from ZAS901G50*05092000 to *05093999.

NO SIGNIFICANT MODIFICATIONS TO THE FOLLOWING MODELS:

Alfasud 1.3 Super (type 901F3B). Chassis from ZAS901F30*05135301 to *05136915
Alfasud ti 1.3 (type 901G4B). Chassis from ZAS901G40*05080901 to *05093999.
Alfasud 1.5 (type 901F4B). Chassis from ZAS901F40*05135301 to *05136915.
Alfasud ti 1.5 (type 901G5B). Chassis from ZAS901G50*05080901 to *05091999.
Alfasud Sprint Veloce 1.3 (type 902A4A) (long ratios). Chassis from ZAS902A40*05090000 to *05092200.
Alfasud Sprint Veloce 1.5 (type 902A5A). Chassis from ZAS902A50*05090000 to *05092200.
Nuova Giulietta L 1.3 (type 116.44). Chassis from ZAR116440*00056500 to*00058900.
Nuova Giulietta L 1.6 (type 116.50B). Chassis from ZAR116500*00136301 to *00159999.
Nuova Giulietta L 1.8 (type 116AA). Chassis from ZAR116A00*00044501 to *00058600.
Alfetta 1.6 (type 116B1A). Chassis from ZAR116B10*00001901 to *00005600.
Alfetta 1.8 (type 116B2). Chassis from ZAR116B20*00001851 to *00005350.
Alfetta 2.0 (type 116.55F). Chassis from ZAR116550*00121101 to *00140500.
Alfetta 2.0 Turbodiesel (type 116B). Chassis from ZAR116B00*00014051 to *00023000.
GTV 2000 (type 116.36C). Chassis from ZAR116360*00055101 to *00062700.
GTV 6 2.5 (type 116C). Chassis from ZAR116C00*00008001 to *00010500.
GTV 6 2.5 with catalytic converter for the U.S. market. **(type 116.69, engine type 01911).** Chassis from ZAR116690*00002001 onwards.
Alfa 6 (type 119A), (type 119A1). No cars produced.
1600 Spider Veloce (type 115.35). No cars produced.
2000 Spider Veloce (type 115.38). Chassis from ZAR115380*02477001 to *02477209.
2000 Spider Veloce injection America (type 115.41). Chassis from ZAR115410*00014001 to *00015230, from ZAR115410*00016001 to *00016199.

COMPETITION CARS NOT FOR PUBLIC SALE
182 (AUTODELTA- DUCAROUGE) - SINGLE-SEATER FORMULA ONE CAR
182 T (AUTODELTA) - SINGLE SEATER FORMULA ONE CAR
ALFASUD SPRINT VELOCE TROFEO (AUTODELTA KIT) - FOR TRACK RACING

1983

SPIDER 1.6
(TYPE 115.35, ENGINE TYPE AR00526A*S)
4 cylinders in line, 1570 cc, 104 hp, twin overhead camshafts. Wheelbase 2250 mm.

Chassis from ZAR115350*00005001 to *00006310.

2000 SPIDER VELOCE
(TYPE 115.38, ENGINE TYPE AR00515)
4 cylinders in line, 1570 cc, 128 hp, twin overhead camshafts, Wheelbase 2250 mm.

Chassis from ZAR115380*02477501 to *02480000. 2000 Spider Veloce injection America (type 115.41). **Chassis from ZAR115410*00016200 to *00017420; from ZAR115410 *00018001 to *00018800.**

PININFARINA ROADSTER

Restyling in inferior taste of the 1983 roadster, which was fitted with wrap around bumpers; the front incorporated a spoiler and flashers while a second aerodynamic device in soft synthetic material was fitted to the tail. The hood was modified and available in black or beige plasticised canvass. Three-spoke steering wheel. Two different engines with no change in performance.

GTV 2000
(TYPE 116.36C, ENGINE TYPE AR01655)

4 cylinders in line, 1962 cc, 130 hp, twin overhead camshafts. Wheelbase 2400 mm.

Chassis from ZAR116360*00062701 to*00066250.

GTV 6 2.5
(TYPE 116CA, ENGINE TYPE AR01646)

V6, 2492 cc, 160 hp, 1 overhead camshaft per main bearing. Wheelbase 2400 mm.

Chassis from ZAR116C00*00012001 to*00015210.
GTV 6 with catalytic converter for the U.S. market (type 116.69, engine type AR01911).
Chassis from ZAR116690*00005001 to.

COUPE'

Following the logic of the general updating, the GTVs were slightly modified: blued windows, lateral protectors in dark grey, aerial incorporated in the windscreen, new sports-type front seats with 'net' headrests and covered with chalk-stripe grey or beige velvet, depending on the colour of the body. Cockpit sound deadening improved by the installation of a parcel panel under the dashboard.

ALFASUD SPRINT QUADRIFOGLIO VERDE

(TYPE 902A5B, ENGINE TYPE AS30146)

ALFASUD SPRINT QUADRIFOGLIO VERDE

(TYPE 902A5C, ENGINE TYPE AS30146)

(long ratios)

4 cylinders horizontally opposed, 1490 cc, 105 hp, single overhead camshaft per main bearing. Wheelbase 2455 mm.

COUPE'

The power of the **Alfasud Sprint** was increased by 10 hp with the modification of the cylinder head, induction and exhaust manifolds, different carburettor calibration and a new setting for the timing system. Maximum speed 180 km/h, acceleration from 0-1000 metres in 31.6 seconds. Inside, seats with net-type headrests and steering wheel rim covered in leather. Externally, alloy wheels, new black wrap around bumpers and a plastic protection side panel. **Chassis from ZAS902A50*05099000 to*05114300.**

GIULIETTA 2.0 TURBODIESEL

(TYPE 116A2, ENGINE TYPE 4HT/2)

4 cylinders in line, 1995 cc, 82 hp, 1 camshaft in crankcase. Wheelbase 2510 mm.

SALOON

The Giulietta was also given a VM diesel engine built at Centro and already, installed in the **Alfetta Turbo Diesel.**
Externally, the car was distinguished by the supplementary air intakes and 165/70 SR 13 tyres. Cockpit sound-deadening was improved by installing additional acoustic insulation panels.

ALFETTA 2.4 TURBO DIESEL
(TYPE 116B3, ENGINE TYPE 4HT/2.4)
4 cylinders in line, 2393 cc, 95 hp, 1 camshaft in crankcase. Wheelbase 2510 mm.

SALOON

Once again a new diesel engine came from Centro's VM, this time a 2.4 diesel, which benefitted from the company's long experience with the 2.0. The cooling system was made more powerful and the much improved performance delivered a 0-1 kilometer acceleration time of 35 seconds. The body and equipment of the whole range included many modifications: radiator grill in ABS, grills for the air intakes and outlets in black, polypropylene bumpers and dark grey molding on the side panels. Electric windows and central locking.
Chassis from ZAR116B30*00001001 to*00008000.

ALFETTA QUADRIFOGLIO ORO
(TYPE 116.55N, ENGINE TYPE AR01713)
4 cylinders in line, 1962 cc, 130 hp, twin overhead camshafts- Wheelbase 2510 mm.

SALOON

The new version was equipped with a sophisticated new electronic ignition and fuel injection system (Bosch Motronic) and with a device for regulating the valve gear timing; this permitted the modification of the regulation in relation to the variation of rotation revolutions. As well as incorporating all the 2.4 TD's modifications, aesthetic variations included: bumpers in the same colour as the body, four round headlights and alloy wheels as original equipment.
Chassis from ZAR116550*00150011 to*00159550.

ALFETTA 1.6
(TYPE 116B1A, ENGINE TYPE AR01600)
4 cylinders in line, 1570 cc, 109 hp, twin overhead camshafts. Wheelbase 2510 mm.

**Chassis from ZAR116B10*00008001
to *00009999.**

ALFETTA 1.8
(TYPE 116B2, ENGINE TYPE AR01678)
4 cylinders in line, 1779 cc, 122 hp, twin overhead camshafts. Wheelbase 2510 mm.

**Chassis from ZAR116B20*00005351
to *00006000, from
ZAR116B20*00008001 to
*00010800.**

ALFETTA 2.0
(TYPE 116.55F, ENGINE TYPE AR1655)
4 cylinders in line, 1962 cc, 130 hp, twin overhead camshafts. Wheelbase 2510 mm.

**Chassis from ZAR116550*00140501
to *00144999, from
ZAR116550*00170001 to
*00176300.**

ALFETTA 2.0 TURBO DIESEL
(TYPE 116BA, ENGINE TYPE 4HT/2)
4 cylinders in line, 1995 cc, 82 hp, 1 camshaft in crankcase. Wheelbase 2510 mm.

**Chassis from ZAR116B00*00025001
to*00026030.**

SALOON

From April, the whole **Alfetta** range
was renewed by applying the
modifications described in the 2.4
TD segment.

ALFA 33 1.3
(TYPE 905A1, ENGINE TYPE AR30502)
4 cylinders horizontally opposed, 1351 cc, 79 hp, 1 overhead camshaft
per main bearing. Wheelbase 2450.

SALOON

With this new front-wheel drive which made its debut in June, Alfa Romeo began to renew its product range. The company planned to invest Lit 1800 billion in the project.
The appearance of the new car was modern and pleasing, even though the finish was rather spartan. The highly successful engine came from the **Alfasud**.
Chassis from ZAR905A10*05001001 to*5063600.

ALFA 33 QUADRIFOGLIO ORO
(TYPE 905A2, ENGINE TYPE AR30504)
4 cylinders horizontally opposed, 1490 cc, 85 hp, 1 overhead camshaft
per main bearing. Wheelbase 2450 mm.

SALOON

The Quadrifoglio Oro was the best model in the 33 range. It was fitted with the 1½ litre engine, which had equipped several of the **Alfasuds** and the performance was very satisfactory. It had headlight washers, brown bumpers, dark side panels, drainage channel covers in black PVC with stainless steel inserts and a passenger door mirror.
Chassis from ZAR905A20*05001001 to*05063600.

NUOVA GIULIETTA 1.6

(TYPE 116.50B, ENGINE TYPE AR01600)

4 cylinders in line, 1570 cc, 109 hp, twin overhead camshafts. Wheelbase 2510 mm.

Chassis from ZAR116500*00160000
to*00181500.

NUOVA GIULIETTA 1.8

(TYPE 116AA, ENGINE TYPE AR01678)

4 cylinders in line, 1779 cc, 122 hp, twin overhead camshafts. Wheelbase 2510 mm.

Chassis from ZAR116A00*00058601
to*00071500.

NUOVA GIULIETTA 2.0 TURBODIESEL

(TYPE 116A2, ENGINE TYPE 4HT/2)

4 cylinders in line, 1995 cc, 82 hp, 1 camshaft in crankcase. Wheelbase 2510 mm.

Chassis from ZAR116A20*00001011
to*00010025.

SALOON

The third series of the Giulietta appeared at the end of the year and benefitted from a careful restyling. The dashboard was completely re-designed and included a box-type oddments compartment. It also had an electronic rev counter and oil pressure dial. The 1.8 and 2.0 TD versions (see engine right) had rear seats with adjustable backs and built-in headrests. Outside, the new 1984 model had: a metallic grey radiator grill (matt black for the 1.6); bumpers without guards but light grey metallic polycarbonate (matt black for the 1.6); protection strip on the lower side panels aligned with the wings. Few mechanical variations: a different induction manifold, new brake servo on the 1.6 and 1.8, none of which changed the car's performance.

ALFA 6 2.0
(TYPE 119A3, ENGINE TYPE AR01932)
60° V6, 1997 cc, 135 hp, 1 overhead camshaft per main bearing.
Wheelbase 2600 mm.

Chassis from ZAR119A30*00001001
to *00001410.

ALFA 6 INJECTION QUADRIFOGLIO ORO
(TYPE 119AA, ENGINE TYPE AR01928)
60° V6, 2492 cc, 158 hp, 1 overhead camshaft per main bearing.
Wheelbase 2600 mm.

Chassis from ZAR119A00*00006001
to*00006400.

ALFA 6 2.5 TURBODIESEL 5
(TYPE 119A2, ENGINE TYPE 5HT/2.5)
5 cylinders in line, 2494 cc, 105 hp, 1 camshaft in crankcase. Wheelbase 2600 mm.

Chassis from ZAR119A20*00001001
to*00002000.

SALOON

Due to its long gestation period, the **Alfa 6** looked somewhat dated. The car was, however, much liked for its refined mechanical qualities, to the point that it was decided to give it a minor re-styling and, for fiscal reasons, produce a less powerful version.

The aesthetic modifications included the elimination of the bumper guards and the headlights became rectangular. Inside, the dash was re-designed as were the new range of seats, which were covered with new materials.

Fuel supply was still by carburettor for the 2.0, while the Injection Quadrifoglio Oro had a Bosch L-Jetronic electronic fuel system identical to that of the GTV 6, instead of the earlier model's six carburettors. By giving up 2 hp, the car returned a noticeable reduction in fuel consumption and exhaust emission was improved. The appearance of the Turbodiesel 5 was the same as the **Alfa 6 2.0** and 2.5; the engine (picture, right) was the new VM 5 cylinder with turbocharger.

NUOVA GIULIETTA 2.0 TURBODELTA
(TYPE 116A1B, ENGINE TYPE ARO1699)
4 cylinders in line, 1962 cc, 170 hp, twin overhead camshafts. Wheelbase 2510 mm.

SALOON

This new weapon with which to conquer the European Touring Car Championship was developed by Autodelta. The new car was to take the place of the GTV 6, whose involvement in the sport was having a diminishing knock-on effect in road car sales. The mechanics were of extremely high level especially developed for racing, and the car revealed itself to even be superior to the **Alfetta GTV Turbodelta**.
But the imminent introduction of the 75 meant the Giulietta Turbodelta never raced. The car was available only in one colour: metallic black with a red stripe

around the entire body. Wrap a round sports-type red seats covered in imitation leather and cloth.
The engine was the classic twin overhead cam with single fuel feed (two twin-choke carburettors) but, thanks to the Alfa Romeo Avio turbocharger elaborated by Autodelta, power went up by 40 hp compared to the standard two litre; the exhaust valves were sodium with stellite inserts; an oil radiator was also added. Self-ventilating disc brakes, a different suspension rating and wheels with five stud bolts.
Chassis from ZAR116A10*00054001 to*00054210.

ARNA L
(TYPE 920A, ENGINE TYPE AR31000)
(3 door)

ARNA SL
(TYPE 920AA, ENGINE TYPE AR31000)
(5 door)
4 cylinders horizontally opposed, 1186 cc, 63 hp, 1 overhead camshaft per main bearing. Wheelbase 2420 mm.

SALOON

The signing of an agreement with Nissan, manufacturer of the Cherry of which the Arna was a close relation, was accompanied by a long controversy over the appropriateness of the operation. The result was, however, acceptable; the **Arna** was a technically successful car

which was not too aesthetically convincing but very effective because it used the highly successful **Alfasud** engine. Almost all the bodyshell, the rear axle, rear drum brakes and the structure of the seats belonged to the Cherry. Available in two versions with either three of five doors and identical technical characteristics. **Chassis from ZAR920A00*05001001 to *05009999.**

ALFA 33 4X4
(TYPE 905A2A, ENGINE TYPE AR30504)
4 cylinders horizontally opposed, 1490 cc, 84 hp, 1 overhead camshaft per main bearing. Wheelbase 2450 mm.

SALOON

Due to the shape of the body, the car lent itself well to four-wheel drive and the result of this development project was optimum. The original rigid axle was simply replaced by Ototrasm of Bari, a specialist four-wheel drive and truck manufacturer. The two-part drive shaft was built by Bierfield. The car was unveiled at the end of the year.
Chassis from ZAR905A20*07001001 to*07001650.

ARNA ti
(TYPE 920A1B, ENGINE TYPE AR31010)
4 cylinders horizontally opposed, 1351 cc, 86 hp, 1 overhead camshaft per main bearing. Wheelbase 2420 mm.

SALOON

A few weeks before the Arna's presentation, the range was broadened by the adoption of the boxer engine of the **Alfasud ti** and Sprint as part of the its normal evolution.
The car had two black spoilers, fog lights and hub caps in black plus a passenger door mirror. The front seats were of new design and the dash was given a new electronic rev counter.
Chassis from ZAR920A10*05001051 to *05009999.

NO SIGNIFICANT MODIFICATIONS TO THE FOLLOWING MODELS:

Alfasud 1.2 S, Alfasud 1.2 SC (type 901D4D). Chassis from ZAS901D40*05447751 to *05454600.

Alfasud 1.3 Super (type 901F3C). Chassis from ZAS901F30*0517000 to *05172000.

Alfasud 1.3 S (type 901F3D). Chassis from ZAS901F30*05170001 to *05172000 (in common with the 1.3 Super).

Alfasud ti 1.3 (type 901G4B). Chassis from ZAS901G40*05094000 to *05102999.

Alfasud ti Quadrifoglio Verde (type 901 G5C). Chassis from ZAS901G50*05094000 to *05102999.

Sprint 1.3 (*) (type 902A4A). Chassis from ZAS902A40*05092201 to *05114300.

Alfasud 1.5 Quadifoglio Oro (type 901F4D). Chassis from ZAS901F40*05170001 to *05172000.

Sprint Veloce 1.5 (*) (type 902A5A). Chassis from ZAS902A50*05092201 to *05098999.

Nuova Giulietta L 1.3 (type 116.44). Chassis from ZAR116440*00058901 to*00059800.

Nuova Giulietta L 1.6 (type 116.50B). Chassis in common with the **Nuova Giulietta 1.6.**

Nuova Giulietta L 1.8 (type 116AA). Chassis in common with the **Nuova Giulietta 1.8.**

Giulietta 2.0 Ti (type 116A1A). Chassis included between ZAR116A10*00021651 and *00027400.

Alfetta 1.6 (type 116B1A) Chassis from ZAR116B10*00005601 to *00005800

Alfetta Quadrifoglio (type 116.55M). Chassis from ZAR116550*00145014 to *00146100.

Alfetta 2.0 Turbodiesel (type 116B). Chassis from ZAR116B00*00023001 to *00024100.

(*) With the arrival of the 33, the Alfasud Sprint Veloce took on the new denomination Sprint, as did the Giulietta Sprint in the mid-Sixties.

COMPETITION CARS NOT FOR PUBLIC SALE
183 T (EURORACING - DUCAROUGE) - SINGLE-SEATER FORMULA ONE CAR
ALFASUD SPRINT VELOCE TROFEO (AUTODELTA KIT) - FOR TRACK RACING

1984

ALFA 33 QUADRIFOGLIO VERDE
(TYPE 905A2D, ENGINE TYPE AS30146)

4 cylinders horizontally opposed, 1490 cc, 105 hp, 1 overhead camshaft per main bearing. Wheelbase 2450 mm.

SALOON

The sports version was introduced a year after the 33 range. The car's performance was superior to the others but the mechanical characteristics contained nothing new as they had been widely used by previous models. There were, however, many aesthetic changes, with many items in black: the radiator grill, front and rear spoilers, the central pillars, the lower door panels and the number plate area.

A thin grey metallic stripe ran the length of the sides; bronze windows and the body available in only two colours, Alfa red and metallic light grey. Tyres were 185/60 R 14 or 190/55 R 340 fitted to 5½ inch wide wheels in sheet steel. Front seats were re-designed and included net-type headrests.

Chassis from ZAR905A20*05076001 to*05143999.

NUOVA GIULIETTA 2.0
(TYPE 116A1A, ENGINE TYPE AR01655)

4 cylinders in line, 1962 cc, 130 hp, twin overhead camshafts. Wheelbase 2510 mm.

SALOON

The new two-litre Giulietta was offered with the characteristics of the Ti and much updated aesthetics: the centre of the bumpers, front grill, guard strips on the tail and air outlet protectors in black, in line with fashion at the time. Bronze-tinted heat proof glass. The car was available in four colours of which three were metallic light grey, musk, opal and the essential Alfa red.

New coverings for the interior.
Chassis from ZAR116A10*00027401 to *00035950.

ALFA 33 4X4
(TYPE 905A2F, ENGINE TYPE AR30520)

4 cylinders horizontally opposed, 1490 cc, 95 hp, 1 overhead camshaft per main bearing. Wheelbase 2450 mm.

SALOON

The 4x4 was given the powerful 95 hp engine.

Chassis from ZAR905A20*07005001 to *07005499.

_ ALFA 33 1.5 GIARDINETTA 4X4 _
(TYPE 905A2B, ENGINE TYPE AR30520)
4 cylinders horizontally opposed, 1490 cc, 95 hp, 1 overhead camshaft
per main bearing. Wheelbase 2455 mm.

STATION WAGON

The new 4x4 finally went on sale in June after its introduction at the Geneva Motor Show, where it attracted considerable interest.
Traction was through the front wheels with the possibility of extending it to the rears. Maximum speed 170 km/h with a 0-1 kilometre acceleration time of 33.1 seconds.
Just two colours available: amaril-lis red and light grey, both metallic, with interior coverings in beige.
Chassis from ZAR905A20*07030001 to *07032250.

ALFA 90 1.8
(TYPE 162A1, ENGINE TYPE AR06202)

4 cylinders in line, 1779 cc, 120 hp, twin overhead camshafts. Wheelbase 2510 mm.

Chassis from ZAR162A10*00001011
to *00002120.

ALFA 90 2.0
(TYPE 162A2, ENGINE TYPE AR06212)

4 cylinders in line, 1962 cc, 128 hp, twin overhead camshafts. Wheelbase 2510 mm.

Chassis from ZAR162A20*00050011
to *00052550.

ALFA 90 2.0 INIEZIONE
(TYPE 162A2A, ENGINE TYPE AR01713)

4 cylinders in line, 1962 cc, 128 hp, twin overhead camshafts. Wheelbase 2510 mm.

Chassis from ZAR162A20*00001011
to *00007000.

ALFA 90 2.5 QUADRIFOGLIO ORO
(TYPE 162A, ENGINE TYPE AR01646)

V6, 2492 cc, 156 hp, 1 overhead camshaft per main bearing. Wheelbase 2510 mm.

Chassis from ZAR162A00*00001011
to *00002799.

ALFA 90 2.4 TD
(TYPE 162A3, ENGINE TYPE 4HT/2.4)

4 cylinders in line, 2393 cc, 110 hp, 1 camshaft in crankcase. Wheelbase 2510 mm.

Chassis from ZAR162A30*00001011
to *00004900.

SALOON

The Alfa 90 was a direct descendent of the **Alfetta**, of which it retained the platform, the refined De Dion rear axle and gearbox and almost all of the remaining mechanics. Even if there was a similarity to the Alfetta, the body design was the result of collaboration with Carrozzeria Bertone, which lauded the design of the previous model.

_ ALFA 33 QUADRIFOGLIO ORO _

(TYPE 905A2G, ENGINE TYPE AR30520)

4 cylinders horizontally opposed, 1490 cc, 95 hp, 1 overhead camshaft
per main bearing. Wheelbase 2450 mm.

SALOON

The power of the Quadrifoglio Oro
was increased by 10 hp so that
only another 10 hp separated it
from the Quadrifoglio Verde.
By this time, they were very
reliable cars; well-built, of a certain
class and were even able to satisfy
fairly demanding customers.
**Chassis from ZAR905A20*05120890
to *05143999.**

ALFA 33 1.3 S

(TYPE 905A1A, ENGINE TYPE AS30168)

4 cylinders horizontally opposed, 1351 cc, 86 hp, 1 overhead camshaft
per main bearing. Wheelbase 2450 mm.

SALOON

To the original 79 hp version with its
twin-choke carburettor was added
a model with a single fuel system
(two-twin choke carburettors) -
practically a carburettor for each
cylinder – which notably improved
efficiency. It was a high performance
engine which was in the Alfasud
Sprint from 1979. The interior was
re-touched: electric front windows
and split rear seat backs.
**Chassis from ZAR905A10*05120890
to*05143999.**

ALFA 33 GIARDINETTA

(TYPE 905A2C, ENGINE TYPE AR30520)

4 cylinders horizontally opposed, 1490 cc, 95 hp, 1 overhead camshaft
per main bearing. Wheelbase 2455 mm.

STATION WAGON

The Giardinetta finally went on
sale and was nothing more than a
front-wheel drive 4x4. Optimum
top speed of 175 km/h for a station
wagon with only a 1500 cc engine.
**Chassis from ZAR905A20*07050001
to *07050999.**

ARNA 1.2 L
(TYPE 920AB, ENGINE TYPE AR30500)
(3 door)

ARNA 1.2 SL
(TYPE 920AC, ENGINE TYPE AR30500)
(5 door)

4 cylinders horizontally opposed, 1186 cc, 68 hp, 1 overhead camshaft per main bearing. Wheelbase 2420 mm.

SALOON

The result of collaboration with Nissan, the Arna controversy continued. An attempt was made to improve the car with a series of initiatives: power was increased and there was a noticeable reduction in fuel consumption, due to its new breakerless ignition. At 90 km/h the Arna returned a consumption of 17.2 km per litre.
Chassis from ZAR920A00*05043001 to *05045900.

NO SIGNIFICANT MODIFICATIONS TO THE FOLLOWING MODELS:

Arna L (type 920A), Arna SL (type 920AA). Chassis from ZAR920A00*05010000 to *05043000.
Arna ti (type 920A1B). Chassis from ZAR920A10*05010000 to *05045900.
Alfa 33 (type 905A1). Chassis from ZAR905A10*05063601 to *05143999.
Alfa 33 Quadrifoglio Oro (type 905A2). Chassis from ZAR905A20*05063601 to *05143999.
Alfa 33 4x4 (type 905A2A). Chassis from ZAR905A20*07001651 to * 07004999.
Sprint 1.3 (type 902A4A). Chassis from ZAS902A40*05114301 to *05120500.
Sprint Quadrifoglio Verde (type A5B e A5C) Chassis from ZAS902A50*05114301 to *05120500.
Nuova Giulietta 1.6 (type 116.50B). Chassis from ZAR116500*00181501 to *00192499.
Nuova Giulietta 1.8 (type 116AA). Chassis from ZAR116A00*00071501 to *00078800.
Nuova Giulietta 2.0 Turbodiesel (type 116A2). Chassis from ZAR116A20*00010026 to *00017100.
Nuova Giulietta 2.0 Turbodelta (type 116A1B). Chassis from ZAR116A10*00054211 to *00054342.
Alfetta 2.0 (type 116.55F). Chassis from ZAR116550*00176301 to *00178350.
Alfetta Quadrifoglio Oro (type 116.55N). Chassis from ZAR116550*00159551 to *00166550.
Alfetta 2.0 Turbo Diesel (type 116BA). Chassis from ZAR116B30*00008001 to *00008800.
Alfetta 2.4 Turbo Diesel (type 116B3). Chassis from ZAR116B00*00026031 to 00026250.
GTV 2000 (type 116.36C). Chassis from ZAR116360*00066251 to *00067850.
GTV 6 2.5 (type 116CA). Chassis from ZAR116C00*00015211 to *00017600.
GTV 6 2.5 with catalytic converter for the U.S. market **(type 116.69, engine type AR01911).** Chassis from ZAR116690*00005501 onwards.
Alfa 6 Injection Quadrifoglio Oro (type 119AA). Chassis from ZAR119A00 *00006401 to *00007000.
Alfa 6 2.0 (type 119A3). Chassis from ZAR119A30 *00001411 to *00002500.
Alfa 6 2.5 Turbodiesel 5 (type 119A2). Chassis from ZAR119A20*00002001 to *00003299.
1600 Spider (type 115.35). Chassis from ZAR115350*00006311 to *00006945.
2000 Spider Veloce (type 115.38). Chassis from ZAR115380*02480001 to *02482250.
2000 Spider Veloce destined for the U.S.A. **(type 115.41).** Chassis from ZAR115410*00018801 to *00021800.

COMPETITION CAR NOT FOR PUBLIC SALE
184 T FORMULA ONE (EURORACING - DUCAROUGE) - SINGLE-SEATER FORMULA ONE CAR

ALFA 75 1.6
(TYPE 162B2A, ENGINE TYPE AR06100)
4 cylinders in line, 1570 cc, 110 hp, twin overhead camshafts. Wheelbase 2510 mm.

**Chassis from ZAR162B20*00001011
to *00011560.**

ALFA 75 1.8
(TYPE 162B1A, ENGINE TYPE AR06202)
4 cylinders in line, 1779 cc, 120 hp, twin overhead camshafts. Wheelbase 2510 mm.

**Chassis from ZAR162B10*00001011
to *00008680.**

ALFA 75 2.0
(TYPE 162BF, ENGINE TYPE AR06212)
4 cylinders in line, 1962 cc, 128 hp, twin overhead camshafts. Wheelbase 2510 mm.

**Chassis from ZAR162B00*00200001
to *00205000.**

ALFA 75 2.0 TURBODIESEL
(TYPE 162BD, ENGINE TYPE VM 80A)
4 cylinders in line, 1995 cc, 95 hp, 1 camshaft in crankcase. Wheelbase 2510 mm.

**Chassis from ZAR162B00*00001011
to *00008200.**

SALOON

The renewal of the range continued and, even if rumours were circulating about the possible acquisition of the company by an overseas manufacturer, the desire to see again the glory of the **Giulietta** of the Fifties and the **Giulia** was evident. The 75 was introduced in May, the 75th anniversary of the establishment of the company; the body design was attractive and the mechanics, direct descendents of the **Alfetta** and **Giulietta**, were optimum. Vanguard performance for the optimisation of mechanics which had been in use for over a decade.

NO SIGNIFICANT MODIFICATIONS TO TO THE FOLLOWING MODELS:

Arna 1.2 L (type 920AB), Arna 1.2 SL (type 920AC). Chassis from ZAR920A00*05045901 to *05056099.

Arna ti (type 920A1B). Chassis from ZAR920A10*05045901 to *05056099.

Alfa 33 1.3 S (type 905A1A). Chassis from ZAR905A10*05144000 to *05203000

Alfa 33 1.5 Quadrifoglio Verde (type 905A2D). Chassis from ZAR905A20*05144000 to *05203000.

Alfa 33 4x4 (type 905A2F). Chassis from ZAR905A20*07005500 to *07006900, from ZAR905A20*05154553 to *05203000.

Alfa 33 Quadrifoglio Oro (type 905A2G). Chassis from ZAR905A20*05144000 to *05203000.

Alfa 33 Quadrifoglio Verde (type 905A2D). Chassis from ZAR905A20*05144000 to *05203000.

Alfa 33 Giardinetta (type 905A2C). Chassis from ZAR905A20*07051000 to *07053700.

Alfa 33 1.5 Giardinetta 4x4 (type 905A2B). Chassis from ZAR905A20*07032251 to *07036510.

Sprint 1.3 (type 902A4A). Chassis from ZAS902A40*05120501 to *05124899.

Sprint Quadrifoglio Verde (type 902A5B, type 902A5C). Chassis from ZAS902A50*05120501 to *05124899.

Nuova Giulietta 1.6 (type 116.50B). Chassis from ZAR116500*00192500 to *00193000.

Nuova Giulietta 1.8 (type 116AA). Chassis from ZAR116A00*00078801 to *00078999.

Nuova Giulietta 2.0 (type 116A1A). Chassis from ZAR116A10*00035951 to *00036300.

Nuova Giulietta 2.0 Turbodiesel (type 116A2). Chassis from ZAR116A20*00017101 to *00018400.

GTV 2000 (type 116.36C). Chassis from ZAR116360*00067851 to *00069000.

GTV 6 2.5 (type 116CA). Chassis from ZAR116C00*00017601 to *00019000.

GTV 6 2.5 with catalytic converter for the U.S. market **(type 116.69, engine type AR01911).** Chassis from ZAR116690*00006411 onwards

Alfa 90 1.8 (type 162A1). Chassis from ZAR162A10*00002121 to *00005999.

Alfa 90 2.0 (type 162A2). Chassis from ZAR162A20*00052551 to *00054299.

Alfa 90 2.0 Iniezione (type 162A2A). Chassis from ZAR162A20*00007001 to *00016199.

Alfa 90 2.5 Quadrifoglio Oro (type 162A). Chassis from ZAR162A00*00002800 to *00006299.

Alfa 90 2.4 TD (type 162A3). Chassis from ZAR162A30*00004901 to *00012250.

Alfa 6 2.0 (type 119A3). Chassis from ZAR119A30 *00002501 to *00002830.

Alfa 6 Injection Quadrifoglio Oro (type 119AA). Chassis from ZAR119A00*00007001 to *00007111.

Alfa 6 Injection Quadrifoglio Oro with automatic gearbox **(type 119AB).** Chassis from ZAR119A00*02002001 to *02002076.

Alfa 6 2.5 Turbodiesel 5 (type 119A2). Chassis from ZAR119A20*00003300 to *00003730.

Spider 1.6 (type 115.35). Chassis from ZAR115350*00006946 to *00007513.

2000 Spider Veloce (type 115.38). Chassis from ZAR115380*02482251 to *02483620.

2000 Spider Veloce destined for the U.S.A. **(type 115.41).** Chassis from ZAR115410*00021801 to *00022039, from ZAR115410*00023001 to *00023950, from ZAR115410*00035011 to *00037500.

COMPETITION CAR NOT FOR PUBLIC SALE
185 T (EURORACING - DUCAROUGE) - SINGLE-SEATER FORMULA ONE CAR

SPIDER 2.0 QUADRIFOGLIO VERDE
(TYPE 115.38, ENGINE TYPE AR00515)
4 cylinders in line, 1962 cc, 128 hp, twin overhead camshafts. Wheelbase 2250 mm.

PININFARINA ROADSTER

Spider 2.0 destined for the U.S.A. (type 115.41). **Chassis from** **ZAR115410*00037501 to *00048800.**

In production for many years, the Alfa Romeo roadster was no longer the only car of its kind on the market. During its lifetime it had been rejuvenated and was given another restyling in time for the Geneva Motor Show.

The Quadrifoglio Verde was introduced with new front and rear spoilers, two new door mirrors and a lateral mini-skirt at the base of the doors. A new hardtop was available as an option and that transformed the car into a comfortable coupè. Of course, the "basic" 1.6 and 2.0 remained in production.
Chassis from ZAR115380*02484011 to*02491159.

ALFA 90 SUPER 1.8
(TYPE 162A1A, ENGINE TYPE AR06202)
4 cylinders in line, 1779 cc, 120 hp, twin overhead camshafts. Wheelbase 2510 mm.

Chassis from ZAR162A10*00006511 to *00007550.

ALFA 90 SUPER 2.0 INIEZIONE
(TYPE 162A2E, ENGINE TYPE AR01713)
4 cylinders in line, 1962 cc, 128 hp, twin overhead camshafts. Wheelbase 2510 mm.

Chassis from ZAR162A20*00017511 to*00018990.

ALFA 90 SUPER 2.5
(TYPE 162AA, ENGINE TYPE AR06210)
V6, 2492 cc, 156 hp, 1 overhead camshaft per main bearing. Wheelbase 2510 mm.

Chassis from ZAR162A00*00007011 to*00007399.

ALFA 90 2.4 SUPER TD
(TYPE 162A3, ENGINE TYPE 4HT/2.4)

4 cylinders in line, 2393 cc, 110 hp, 1 camshaft in crankcase. Wheelbase 2510 mm.

Chassis from ZAR162A30*00012251 to*00016300.

SALOON

The 90 had been negatively affected by the launch and success of the 75. To give it back some credibility, Alfa Romeo carried out a mild restyling and mechanical updating. As a result, five different models in the Super series were introduced and they substituted the previous series. The 2.0 with carburettor was withdrawn.
Pick-up times were improved 20%-

25%; ABS was offered for the first time on the 6 cylinder version. The 90 Super had a new-design radiator grill with chrome shield and a new finish for the bumpers and under-door panels. New seat coverings and more comfort in general. New range of colours.

ALFA 90 SUPER 2.0 V6 INIEZIONE
(TYPE 162 A2D, ENGINE TYPE AR06210)

V6, 1996 cc, 132 hp, 1 overhead camshaft per main bearing. Wheelbase 2510 mm.

SALOON

The Alfa 90 series also adopted the V6 engine, but with its power reduced to two litres to avoid 38% purchase tax levied on a more powerful car. Equipment was generally the same as the 2.5 Quadrifoglio Oro and included all the updates carried out to create the Super range.
Chassis from ZAR162A20*00105011 to *00106400.

ALFA 75 2.5 V6 QUADRIFOGLIO VERDE
(TYPE 162B3, ENGINE TYPE AR01646)

V6, 2492 cc, 156 hp, 1 overhead camshaft per main bearing. Wheelbase 2510 mm.

SALOON

The V6 engine, a masterpiece of Arese engineering, also equipped the Alfa 75. The car was fun to drive, delivered a far superior performance to its competitors and imbued Alfa Romeo once again with the sportiness for which it had become famous.
Chassis from ZAR162B30*00001011 to *00003113.

ALFA 75 1.8i TURBO
(TYPE 162B1C, ENGINE TYPE AR06134)
4 cylinders in line, 1779 cc, 155 hp, twin overhead camshafts. Wheelbase 2510 mm.

SALOON

Succumbing to the fashion for turbocharged engines which had raged through Europe, Alfa Romeo decided to fit a turbo to its 75, exploiting its past experience with the GTV Turbodelta and its racing cars. The turbo was a Garrett T3 fitted with a special cooling system; modifications to the engine were limited to the small number of adjustments, partly because, since the time of the **Giulietta** in 1954, it had been adapted with "damp tubes" which were completely immersed in refrigerating liquid. So the Alfa two-litre was able to disperse well the typical thermic increases generated by a turbo. Aesthetically, few variations: extended edges for the wings, wider wheels, bumpers the same colour as the body.
Chassis from ZAR162B10*00050011 to*00054249.

ALFA 33 1.3
(TYPE 905A1B, ENGINE TYPE AR30502)
4 cylinders horizontally opposed, 1351 cc, 79 hp, 1 overhead camshaft per main bearing. Wheelbase 2450 mm.

ALFA 33 1.3 S
(TYPE 905A1C, ENGINE TYPE AS30168)
4 cylinders horizontally opposed, 1351 cc, 86 hp, 1 overhead camshaft per main bearing. Wheelbase 2450 mm.

Chassis from ZAR905A10*05230201 to*05275999 (both models).

ALFA 33 1.5 ti
(TYPE 905A2H, ENGINE TYPE AS30146)

ALFA 33 1.5 4X4
(TYPE 905A2L, ENGINE TYPE AS30146)

4 cylinders horizontally opposed, 1490 cc, 105 hp, 1 overhead camshaft per main bearing. Wheelbase 2450 mm.

Chassis from ZAR905A20*05230201 to*05275999 (both models).

ALFA 33 1.5 GIARDINETTA
(TYPE 905A2N, ENGINE TYPE AS 30146)

ALFA 33 1.5 GIARDINETTA 4X4
(TYPE 905A2M, ENGINE TYPE AS30146)

4 cylinders horizontally opposed, 1490 cc, 105 hp, 1 overhead camshaft per main bearing. Wheelbase 2450 mm; 4x4 2455 mm.

Chassis from ZAR905A20*05230201 to*05275999 (both models).

SALOON AND STATION WAGON
Towards the end of the year, the new 33 took the place of the old. Aesthetic modifications affected the radiator grill and hub caps of different design, while the rear optical groups and indicator flashers became white.
The 1.3 S, with single fuel system (two twin-choke carburettors), was also named "Boxer".
Performance generally superior to the previous model.

ALFA 33 1.7 QUADRIFOGLIO VERDE
(TYPE 905A3, ENGINE TYPE AR30550)

4 cylinders horizontally opposed, 1712 cc, 118 hp, 1 overhead camshaft per main bearing. Wheelbase 2480 mm.

SALOON

New to the 33 range was the 1.7 Quadrifoglio Verde, a car of greater sporting character with spoilers front and rear, front windows with anti-turbulence deflectors and door ledges joined to the front and rear wings with mini-skirts, in line with the fashion of the period. The increase in cubic capacity was easily absorbed by the robust boxer engine, the optimisation of which had been non-stop, and was achieved by increasing the bore and stroke (87x72).
Aesthetic changes were in line with the rest of the new range.
Chassis from ZAR905A30*05230201 to *05275999.

ALFA 33 1.8 TURBODIESEL

(TYPE 905A4, ENGINE TYPE VM 82A)

ALFA 33 1.8 TURBODIESEL GIARDINETTA

(TYPE 905A4A, ENGINE TYPE VM 82A)

3 cylinders in line, 1779 cc, 74 hp, 1 camshaft in the crankcase. Wheelbase 2460 mm.

SALOON AND STATION WAGON

An new and interesting 3 cylinder diesel engine was built by VM of Centro, Ferrara, a member company of the IRI Meccanica group and Alfa's partner in the production of diesel engines: it equipped both versions of the new 33 turbodiesel, the saloon and station wagon.
Performance was good, with a maximum speed of 165 km/h.

Aesthetic changes were in line with the rest of the new range.
Chassis from ZAR905A40*05230201 **to *05275999 (both models).**

NO SIGNIFICANT MODIFICATIONS TO THE FOLLOWING MODELS:
Arna 1.2 L (type 920AB), Arna 1.2 SL (type 920 AC). Chassis from ZAR920A00*05056100 to *05061100.
Arna ti (type 920A1B). Chassis from ZAR920A10*05056100 to *05061100.
Alfa 33 1.3 (type 905A1A). Chassis from ZAR905A10*05203001 to *05230200.
Alfa 33 4x4 (type 905A2F). Chassis from ZAR905A20*05203001 to *05230200.
Alfa 33 Quadrifoglio Oro (type 905A2G). Chassis from ZAR905A20*05203001 to *05230200.
Alfa 33 Quadrifoglio Verde (type 905A2D). Chassis from ZAR905A20*05203001 to *05230200.
Alfa 33 Giardinetta (type 905A2C). Chassis from ZAR905A20*05208697 to *05230200, from
ZAR905A20*07053701 to *07054600.
Alfa 33 1.5 Giardinetta 4x4 (type 905A2B). Chassis from ZAR905A20*05208151 to *05230200, from
ZAR905A20*07036511 to *07037700
Sprint 1.3 (type 902A4A). Chassis from ZAS902A40*05124900 to *05128600.
Sprint Quadrifoglio Verde (type 902A5B and type 902A5C). Chassis from ZAS902A50*05124900 to *05128600.
Alfa 90 2.0 Iniezione (type 162A2A). Chassis from ZAR162A20*00016200 to *00017510.
Alfa 90 2.4 Turbodiesel (type 162A3). Chassis from ZAR162A30*00012251 to *00016300.
Alfa 75 1.6 (type 162B2A). Chassis from ZAR162B20*00011561 to *00035500.
Alfa 75 1.8 (type 162B1A). Chassis from ZAR162B10*00008681 to *00021800.
Alfa 75 2.0 (type 162BF). Chassis from ZAR162B00*00205001 to *00215399.
Alfa 75 2.0 Turbodiesel (type 162BD). Chassis from ZAR162B00*00008201 to *00017600.
GTV 6 2.5 (type 116CA). Chassis from ZAR116C00*00020040 to *00020400.
GTV 6 2.5 with catalytic converter destined for the U.S.A. and Germany **(type 116.69, engine type 01911).** Chassis from ZAR116690*00007501 onwards.
Spider 1600 (type 115.35). Chassis from ZAR115350*00008001 to *00008750.

Printed in Italy by
Poligrafiche Bolis, Bergamo
October, 2000.